Dajuana McCloud

MW00787540

# PACEMAKER®

# World History

# WORKBOOK

RIVERSIDE COUNTY
OFFICE OF EDUCATION
3939 13th ST.
P.O. BOX 868
RIVERSIDE, CA 92502-0868

Globe
Fearon

Parsippany, New Jersey
www.pearsonlearning.com

# Pacemaker® World History Fourth Edition

Reviewer
We thank the following educator, who provided valuable comments and suggestions during the development of this book:

*Pacemaker Curriculum Advisor:* Stephen C. Larsen, formerly of the University of Texas at Austin

**Project Staff**
Executive Editor: Jane Petlinski
Project Manager: Suzanne Keezer
Lead Designer: Janice Noto-Helmers
Manufacturing Buyer: Nathan Kinney

**About the Cover**
*World History* is the study of important people, places, and events of the world. The images on the cover represent the history and culture of the world's regions. The large image in the center is the statue of the Egyptian pharaoh, Rameses II. On the left, from top to bottom, are an Aztec calendar; a ceremonial mask from Africa; and a Japanese fan. On the right, from top to bottom, are a modern-day astronaut; a Portuguese astrolabe, which was used to find the altitude of stars; and a decorative box from Russia. If you were to make a time capsule of the present day, what objects from your culture or region would you include?

Copyright © 2002 by Pearson Education Inc., publishing as Globe Fearon, an imprint of Pearson Learning, 299 Jefferson Road, Parsippany, NJ 01054. All rights reserved. No part of this book may be reproduced or transmitted in any form or by any means, electronic, photographic, mechanical, or otherwise including photocopying, recording, or by any information storage and retrieval system, without permission in writing from the publisher.

ISBN: 0-130-238-31-7

Printed in the United States of America

5  6  7  8  9  10      05  04

Globe Fearon
Pearson Learning Group

1-800-321-3106
www.pearsonlearning.com

# Contents

# A Note to the Student

The exercises in this workbook go along with your *Pacemaker World History* textbook. Each exercise in this workbook is linked to a chapter in your textbook. This workbook gives you the opportunity to do three things—review, practice, and think critically.

The review exercises are questions and activities that test your knowledge of the information presented in the textbook. Set goals for yourself and try to meet them as you complete each activity. Being able to remember and apply information is an important skill, and leads to success on tests, in school, at work, and in life.

The skill practice exercises help you to apply social studies skills. You will need these skills as you read and write about the information you have learned in your textbook. Some pages in the workbook have charts, graphs, maps, and timelines. These pages will give you extra practice in using these skills.

Your critical thinking skills are challenged when you complete the critical thinking exercises. Critical thinking— or to put it another way, thinking critically—means putting information to use. For example, you may review and recall information about how people in early civilizations lived and worked. Later you might use that information to explain how the world came to be the way it is today. When you apply what you know to a different situation, you are thinking critically.

Your textbook is a wonderful source of knowledge. By using it along with this workbook, you will learn a great deal about economics. The real value of the information will come when you have mastered the skills and put them to use by thinking critically.

Name _____  Date _____

 **1 ▶ Categorizing Source Materials**                    **Exercise 1**

When putting together a history, people often use primary sources for their information. A primary source can be a person who was actually present at an event. The primary source can be a letter, a journal, or some other document written at the time. It can be the writings on the walls of a cave or pyramid. Artifacts from a certain time period or civilization are also primary sources. These sources can be hundreds of years old or a few years old. Sometimes pictures can be primary sources. Historians use old photographs to tell what people looked like, how they dressed, and how they lived.

Historians also use secondary sources for information. A secondary source provides information from someone who was not actually a part of an event but knows something about it. A secondary source might be a book written about an event. A secondary source might be someone who was not present at an event but remembers people telling about it. Your history book is a secondary source of information for you.

**Historians might use any of the following listed sources for information. Decide if each one is a primary or a secondary source. Write *primary* or *secondary* on the line before each item.**

_____ **1.** a letter from Napoleon to his wife Josephine

_____ **2.** a book written in 2000 which is called *A Brief History of Early Europe*

_____ **3.** a journal kept by Christopher Columbus

_____ **4.** war memories of a veteran of World War II

_____ **5.** stories about World War I told by the granddaughter of a World War I veteran

_____ **6.** the picture-covered walls of an Egyptian tomb

_____ **7.** the *Emancipation Proclamation* written in Abraham Lincoln's own hand

_____ **8.** a summary of the content of Lincoln's *Emancipation Proclamation*

_____ **9.** a photograph of World War II bombing damage in London

_____ **10.** a recording of a speech given by Winston Churchill

_____ **11.** an Egyptian mummy

_____ **12.** a book on Egyptian pyramids written by a famous archaeologist

_____ **13.** the original map of ancient Greece

_____ **14.** the drawing of a Viking ship

_____ **15.** the original copy of the United States' Declaration of Independence

© Pearson Education, Inc., publishing as Globe Fearon. All rights reserved.

**1 ▶ Writing a History**

**A.** List some events that are part of your own history. (Think about major experiences that have made you the person you are today.)

_____

_____

_____

_____

_____

_____

_____

**B.** Now list some events that took place in your family before you were born. (You can focus on your parents' generation or go back further in your family's history.)

_____

_____

_____

_____

_____

_____

**C.** Choose the event you consider the most interesting. Write a one- or two-paragraph description of the event on a separate sheet of paper.

© Pearson Education, Inc., publishing as Globe Fearon. All rights reserved.

# 1 ▶ Making a Timeline

Exercise 3

*Skill Practice*

**A.** Historians often describe the earliest humans in terms of the tools
and weapons they used in their daily lives. Read the following
descriptions of the early eras of the human race. Then complete
the following timeline.

| | |
|---|---|
| **100,000** B.C. | **Beginning of Old Stone Age**<br>People made crude weapons and tools of stone and wood. |
| **8,000** B.C. | **Beginning of New Stone Age**<br>People made more advanced tools and weapons of stone and wood. |
| **4,000** B.C. | **Beginning of Bronze Age**<br>People began to use copper and bronze tools and weapons. |
| **1,500** B.C. | **Beginning of Iron Age**<br>People began to use iron tools and weapons. |

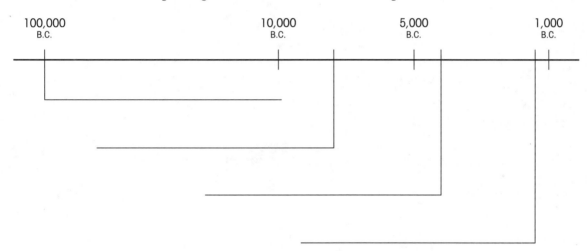

**B.** Number each item below in the order in which it took place. Use
the information on this page and on the timeline found on page
22 of your textbook.

_____ **A.** People began making pottery.

_____ **B.** People began making tools of bronze.

_____ **C.** Humans began to tame animals to help them in their work.

_____ **D.** The Ice Age ended.

_____ **E.** The Old Stone Age began.

© Pearson Education, Inc., publishing as Globe Fearon.
All rights reserved.

## 2 ▷ Using a Map

**A.** Use the text on pages 20–22 and the maps on page 23 of your
textbook to answer the following questions.

1. The map of the Middle East now shows that the Nile River runs through which country?

   _____

2. The Tigris and Euphrates rivers run through which three modern nations?

   _____, _____, and _____

3. A land that was once called Anatolia is now what nation? _____

4. The Sinai Peninsula is in what modern-day country? _____

5. The site of the ancient land of Sumer is in what modern-day country?

   _____

6. In ancient days, the Tigris and Euphrates rivers flowed into what body of water?

   _____

   What is that body of water called today? _____

7. The Fertile Crescent includes lands that are now known as what eight countries?

   _____, _____, _____,

   _____, _____, _____,

   _____, _____

**B.** Early farming civilizations developed in the ancient Middle East.
The area became known as the "Cradle of Civilization." Events in
the Middle East are of great importance today. Find a newspaper
article describing current events in one of the places shown on the
modern map on page 23. Read the news story. Then write a one-
paragraph summary of its content on a separate sheet of paper.

© Pearson Education, Inc., publishing as Globe Fearon.
All rights reserved.

Name _____    Date _____

 **Becoming an Inventor**                          **Exercise 5**

Suppose that you are one of the early human beings. You are curious
and clever. You have just discovered or invented one of the items
named below. You must present the item to your people and convince
them it is of great value. Choose one of the inventions or discoveries,
and write one or two paragraphs explaining its value and importance.

   **1.** You have discovered fire.

   **2.** You have tamed a dog.

   **3.** You have invented the wheel.

   **4.** You have made the first clay pot.

   **5.** You have invented a wood plow.

   **6.** You have discovered that if you dig a ditch leading from a stream to a field, water
   will flow to your crops.

_____

_____

_____

_____

_____

_____

_____

_____

_____

_____

_____

_____

_____

_____

© Pearson Education, Inc., publishing as Globe Fearon.
All rights reserved.

## 3 ▶ Using a Code: The Invention of Writing  **Exercise 6**

*Critical Thinking*

The following six characters were used as cuneiform symbols in about 3000 B.C.

Sun　　　　God, Heaven　　Mountain　　　　　　Man　　　　　　　Ox　　　　Fish

Write a sentence for each of the characters. Draw the character instead of writing the word.

**For example**

As soon as the ◇ rose in the sky, we knew it was going to be a very hot day.

　　　　　　　Sun

1. _____

_____

2. _____

_____

3. _____

_____

4. _____

_____

5. _____

_____

6. _____

_____

© Pearson Education, Inc., publishing as Globe Fearon. All rights reserved.

# 3 ▶ Identifying Fact and Opinion

**Exercise 7**

*Skill Practice*

**A.** A fact is a statement that can be proven true or false. A statement of opinion, on the other hand, tells what someone believes about something. It may show approval or disapproval. Decide whether each statement is a fact or an opinion. Write *F* for Fact or *O* for Opinion beside each sentence.

_____ **1.** Sumerian farmers were hard-working people.

_____ **2.** The Sumerians dug canals and built dikes.

_____ **3.** People of today should appreciate the gifts the Sumerians gave to the world.

_____ **4.** The Sumerians used reeds as pens and drew on clay tablets.

_____ **5.** Wealthy Sumerians were happier than poor Sumerians.

_____ **6.** Only boys attended Sumerian schools.

_____ **7.** The Sumerians should have allowed girls to attend school.

_____ **8.** The Sumerian schools were too strict.

_____ **9.** Sumerian cities were invaded by Babylonians.

_____ **10.** The Babylonians should not have destroyed the Sumerian cities.

**B.** Sumerian villages and city-states are described on pages 31 and 32 in your textbook. In the space below, draw your own sketch of a Sumerian village or city-state.

© Pearson Education, Inc., publishing as Globe Fearon. All rights reserved.

# 3 ▶ Defining Words                                    Exercise 8

**A.** Write a definition for each of the following words. You may review
Chapter 3 in your textbook and use a dictionary if you need help.

**1.** plow _____

**2.** ziggurat _____

**3.** cuneiform _____

**4.** archaeologist _____

**5.** temple _____

**6.** irrigation _____

**7.** city-state _____

**B.** Suppose that you were living in Sumer in 3000 B.C. Write a two- or
three-paragraph journal entry describing a typical day. Begin by
telling your station in life, your gender, and your age. Use
information from Chapter 3 and the timeline on page 37 in your
textbook to help you. Continue writing on a separate sheet of paper.

I am _____

Dear Diary,

    Today _____

_____

_____

_____

_____

_____

_____

_____

© Pearson Education, Inc., publishing as Globe Fearon.
All rights reserved.

Name _____   Date _____

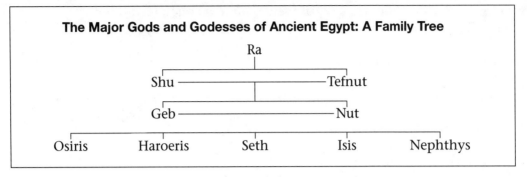

**The Major Gods and Godesses of Ancient Egypt: A Family Tree**

| Name | Description |
|------|-------------|
| Ra | the creator; the sun god; also called Re, Ra-Atum |
| Shu | god of sunlight and air |
| Tefnut | goddess of moisture; also called the "eye of Ra" |
| Geb | the earth god |
| Nut | the sky goddess; can appear in the form of a cow |
| Osiris | god of the underworld; husband and brother of Isis |
| Seth | god of chaos |
| Isis | goddess of magical power; wife and sister of Osiris |
| Nephthys | goddess of burials |

**Choose the one best answer to each item.**

1. According to the family tree of the gods and goddesses, the first god was

    **(a)** Nephthys.   **(b)** Ra.   **(c)** Osiris.

2. The two children of the first god were

    **(a)** Osiris and Isis.   **(b)** Geb and Nut.   **(c)** Shu and Tefnut.

3. The creator god Ra is connected with the

    **(a)** moon.   **(b)** sun.   **(c)** stars.

4. The Egyptian god of the underworld is

    **(a)** Isis.   **(b)** Nephthys.   **(c)** Osiris.

5. Which goddess could appear in the form of a cow?

    **(a)** Nut   **(b)** Isis   **(c)** Nephthys

© Pearson Education, Inc., publishing as Globe Fearon. All rights reserved.

# 4 ▶ Drawing Conclusions                    Exercise 10

*Critical Thinking*

Each group of facts in Column A should lead you to a conclusion
listed in Column B. Match each group of facts with a conclusion.

**Column A**                                          **Column B**

_____ **1.** The Egyptians built great towering tombs
known as pyramids. They filled the tombs
with treasures. They followed an elaborate
procedure of mummifying dead bodies.

                                                                            **a.** The Egyptians were an
inventive people.

_____ **2.** The Egyptians came up with a system of
picture-writing called hieroglyphics. They
built ships. They learned to make paper
called papyrus.

                                                                            **b.** A source of water is
important to the success
of a civilization.

_____ **3.** Pharaohs collected huge taxes from their
people. They lived rich, splendid lives.
They were buried in huge pyramids.

                                                                            **c.** The Egyptians were very
concerned with death
and afterlife.

_____ **4.** The walls of Egyptian tombs were often
covered with hieroglyphics. Artifacts of
ancient life were found in many tombs.
Well-preserved mummies were taken from
some of the tombs.

                                                                            **d.** The pharaohs were
powerful rulers who
commanded great shows
of respect.

_____ **5.** The Egyptians built a civilization along the
Nile. The Nile River flooded each year,
leaving the lands around it fertile.
Egyptian farmers learned to dig canals
from the Nile to irrigate their lands.

                                                                            **e.** Egyptian tombs are rich
sources of historical
information.

© Pearson Education, Inc., publishing as Globe Fearon. All rights reserved.

# 4 ▶ Comparing Civilizations

**Exercise 11**

In Chapter 3, you read about the ancient Sumerian civilization. In Chapter 4, you read about the ancient Egyptians. Each of the following descriptions applies to at least one of these civilizations. Some apply to both civilizations. Read each statement. Then beside each number, write either *S* for *Sumerian,* *E* for *Egyptian,* or *S & E* for both.

_____ **1.** The farmers found ways to irrigate their crops by digging canals from the river to the field.

_____ **2.** City-states were built around gigantic temples called ziggurats.

_____ **3.** The people invented a form of picture-writing called hieroglyphics.

_____ **4.** The people invented a symbol-writing called cuneiform.

_____ **5.** Ships were built for trading.

_____ **6.** Powerful rulers were known as pharaohs.

_____ **7.** Farmers had to pay taxes.

_____ **8.** Artists made fine jewelry.

_____ **9.** The people believed that when they died, they went to another world.

_____ **10.** Workers built huge tombs called pyramids.

_____ **11.** Each city had its own special god.

_____ **12.** Osiris was worshiped as the powerful god of death.

_____ **13.** Archaeologists have pieced together history from objects found in graves and tombs.

_____ **14.** The people made a paper called papyrus from reeds that grew by the river.

© Pearson Education, Inc., publishing as Globe Fearon. All rights reserved.

# 5 ▶ Comparing Civilizations                     Exercise 12

**A.** In Chapter 5, you read about several different Mediterranean civilizations. Each of the following items relates to one of those civilizations. Write the code letter for each civilization next to each item.

Hebrew = He        Babylonian = B        Assyrian = A

Phoenician = Ph     Hittite = Hi

_____ **1.** an alphabet like ours today

_____ **2.** siege engines

_____ **3.** the Tower of Babel

_____ **4.** the Ten Commandments

_____ **5.** the Jewish religion

_____ **6.** the city of Ashur

_____ **7.** a code of laws

_____ **8.** Tyrian purple dye

_____ **9.** belief in one God

_____ **10.** hanging gardens

_____ **11.** cities of Tyre, Sidon, Byblos

_____ **12.** the Promised Land

_____ **13.** navigation

_____ **14.** iron weapons

_____ **15.** city of Babylon

**B.** Match each of the following people on the left with their description on the right. Write the correct letter on the line.

_____ **1.** Abraham        **a.** a Philistine giant

_____ **2.** Hammurabi      **b.** a Hebrew shepherd who fought a giant

_____ **3.** Moses          **c.** a great king of Babylonia

_____ **4.** Goliath        **d.** a wise Hebrew king of Jerusalem

_____ **5.** David          **e.** the father of the Hebrew people

_____ **6.** Solomon        **f.** the Hebrew who led his people out of Egypt

© Pearson Education, Inc., publishing as Globe Fearon. All rights reserved.

Name _____     Date _____

 **5 ▶ Making a Chart**                                **Exercise 13**

*Skill Practice*

Complete the following chart by listing the gifts each civilization left
for humanity. You may review Chapters 3, 4, and 5 to help you
complete the chart.

## Gifts to the World

**Sumerian**

_____

_____

_____

_____

_____

**Egyptian**

_____

_____

_____

_____

_____

**Phoenician**

_____

_____

_____

_____

**Hebrew**

_____

_____

_____

_____

**Babylonian**

_____

_____

_____

_____

**Assyrian**

_____

_____

_____

_____

© Pearson Education, Inc., publishing as Globe Fearon.
All rights reserved.

# 5 ▶ Putting Events in Order

Exercise 14

**A. Number the following events in the order they occurred.**
**(Remember that when using B.C. dates, the lower numbers are**
**more recent. For example, 100 B.C. is more recent than 1500 B.C.)**

_____ **A.** 1240 B.C.—Moses leads Hebrews out of Egypt

_____ **B.** 1100 B.C.—Phoenicians rise to power

_____ **C.** 573  B.C.—Phoenician city of Tyre is conquered

_____ **D.** 722  B.C.—Assyrians conquer Israel

_____ **E.** 587  B.C.—Babylonians take Jerusalem

_____ **F.** 2000 B.C.—Beginning of Babylonian Empire

_____ **G.** 1792 B.C.—Hammurabi begins rule of Babylonia

_____ **H.** 1650 B.C.—Beginning of Hittite Empire

_____ **I.** 1200 B.C.—Hittites conquered by Sea People; Beginning of
Assyrian Empire

_____ **J.** 612  B.C.—End of Assyrian Empire

**B. Use information from the list above to answer these questions.**

1.  Which empire is older, the Babylonian or the Hittite? _____

2.  What happened the same year that the Hittites were conquered by the Sea People?

    _____

3.  What event happened in 1240 B.C.? _____

4.  In 600 B.C., the Phoenicians probably sailed around Africa. How many years later was

    the Phoenician city of Tyre conquered? _____

5.  Hammurabi ruled the Babylonians until 1750 B.C. For how many years did he rule?

    _____

6.  The Assyrian Empire began to break up in 670 B.C. How many years later did it fall?

    _____

© Pearson Education, Inc., publishing as Globe Fearon. All rights reserved.

# 6 ▶ Summarizing Historical Topics

## Exercise 15

*Critical Thinking*

Write a brief paragraph that summarizes each of the topics listed below. If you need more room, continue writing on a separate sheet of paper.

1. The Aryan caste system

   _____

   _____

   _____

   _____

2. The Great Wall of China

   _____

   _____

   _____

   _____

3. Buddhist beliefs

   _____

   _____

   _____

   _____

4. A land bridge to the Americas

   _____

   _____

   _____

   _____

© Pearson Education, Inc., publishing as Globe Fearon. All rights reserved.

Name _____   Date _____

Each of the following subjects relates to one of the topic headings.
Write each subject on a line under the correct heading. (Hint: Some
subjects may be used more than once.)

| | |
|---|---|
| Aryan conquerors | Mohenjo-Daro |
| caste system | maize |
| dynasties | Olmecs |
| Huang He | Siddhartha Gautama |
| Confucius | Maya |
| Asoka | raja |

**India**

_____

_____

_____

_____

_____

**China**

_____

_____

_____

_____

_____

**Buddhism**

_____

_____

_____

_____

_____

**The Americas**

_____

_____

_____

_____

_____

© Pearson Education, Inc., publishing as Globe Fearon. All rights reserved.

## 6 ▶ Making a Timeline

**A.** Place each of the events listed in the correct place on the timeline.

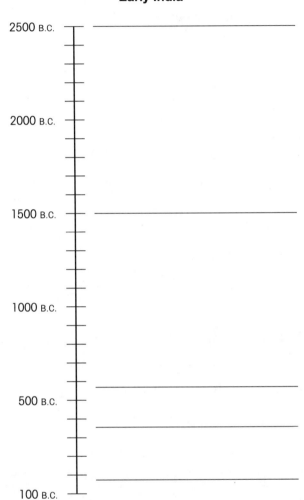

**Early India**

Siddhartha Gautama is born, 563 B.C.

Maurya Empire begins, 321 B.C.

Indus Valley civilization, 2500 B.C.

Aryan invasions, 1500 B.C.

Maurya Empire ends, 185 B.C.

© Pearson Education, Inc., publishing as Globe Fearon.
All rights reserved.

**B.** Use the timeline to answer these questions.

1. The Great Wall of China was begun during the Qin dynasty between 221 and 206 B.C. Was that *before* or *after* the Maurya Empire began?

   _____

2. Confucius was born in 551 B.C. Was that *before* or *after* the birth of Siddhartha

   Gautama? _____

3. The Olmec civilization began in America in 1200 B.C. Was that *before* or *after* the

   Aryan invasion of the Indus River Valley? _____

**7 ▶ Identifying Point of View**                    **Exercise 18**

**A.** A point of view is a certain way of looking at a situation. A person's beliefs, attitudes, and opinions depend largely on that person's point of view. Point of view is affected by one's past experiences. For example, a citizen of Sparta would have viewed life differently than a citizen of Athens.

Decide if each of the following statements would have most likely been made by a Spartan or an Athenian. In other words, identify the point of view of each statement. Write *S* for *Spartan* or *A* for *Athenian* beside each statement.

_____ **1.** Male children are of great value to the city-state. Females are of little use.

_____ **2.** Our beautiful Parthenon stands atop the Acropolis.

_____ **3.** Our military power is our most important asset!

_____ **4.** Art, music, and drama—these are the beauties of life.

_____ **5.** We must take time to ask questions about our world, to wonder about good and evil.

_____ **6.** A baby boy born with something wrong will only weaken our society and has no reason to live.

_____ **7.** Our constitution will give all free men the rights of citizenship.

_____ **8.** We will use our strength to cut off our enemy's supplies and starve their people.

**B.** Choose *one* of the pairs listed below. Write one paragraph that compares similarities between the two. Write a second paragraph that contrasts the pair's differences. Write your paragraphs on a separate sheet of paper.

**1.** the Athenian constitution, the United States Constitution

**2.** the Olympic games of Ancient Greece, modern Olympic Games

© Pearson Education, Inc., publishing as Globe Fearon. All rights reserved.

# 7 ▶ Using a Chart

| The Major Gods and Goddesses of Ancient Greece | |
| --- | --- |
| **Name** | **Description** |
| Zeus | king of the gods; lord of the sky |
| Hera | queen of the gods; protector of married women |
| Poseidon | god of the sea; brother of Zeus; gave humanity the horse |
| Hades | god of the underworld; brother of Zeus |
| Demeter | goddess of grain |
| Persephone | daughter of Zeus and Demeter; wife of Hades |
| Aphrodite | goddess of love and beauty; born from the sea on a bed of foam |
| Apollo | god of the sun; god of music and song; taught mortals the art of healing |
| Ares | god of war |
| Artemis | goddess of the moon; the huntress |
| Dionysus | god of wine |
| Hephaestus | god of metalworkers and craftworkers; forged the armor of the gods; Aphrodite's husband |
| Hermes | Zeus's messenger; god of thieves; wore winged hat and sandals |

© Pearson Education, Inc., publishing as Globe Fearon. All rights reserved.

**Use information from the chart to choose the one best answer to each item.**

1. The king of the gods was

    (a) Hephaestus.    (b) Poseidon.    (c) Zeus.

2. His queen was

    (a) Aphrodite.    (b) Hera.    (c) Demeter.

3. The king of the gods had two brothers. They were

    (a) Ares and Apollo.    (b) Hades and Dionysus.    (c) Hades and Poseidon.

4. Poseidon was

    (a) god of the sea.    (b) god of the underworld.    (c) god of the sun.

5. When Zeus wanted to deliver a message, he would send

    (a) Artemis.    (b) Hermes.    (c) Hephaestus.

6. Aphrodite's husband worked at

    (a) making armor for the gods.    (b) making rain.    (c) teaching mortals the art of healing.

Name _____   Date _____

# 7 ▶ Interpreting Information

## Exercise 20

**A. Read the following article. Then answer the statements. If it is true write *T*. If it is false write *F*.**

---

### The Death of Socrates

Socrates was one of the greatest of the Greek philosophers. He spent his time teaching the men of Athens. He believed it was his duty to lead them to a nobler life. Socrates left behind no writings of his own. His wisdom comes to us through the writings of his student, Plato.

Socrates argued that no person is really bad, but he or she is only unaware of the truths of life. Socrates was not afraid to be unpopular. He refused to give up his principles, even when they went against general opinions. Athenian leaders saw Socrates as a threat to their rule. In 399 B.C. Socrates was charged with introducing new gods and not worshiping the old gods. He was also charged with corrupting the youth of Athens with his teachings. When Socrates stood trial, he insisted on acting as his own lawyer. Socrates was found guilty and sentenced to die.

The great philosopher spent his last hours talking with friends. When night came, he drank a poisonous brew made from hemlock. Socrates lifted his cup of poison in a toast to the gods. Then he lay down on his bed and died.

---

_____ **1.** Socrates believed that some people are born good while others are born evil.

_____ **2.** Socrates was popular with the Athenian government.

_____ **3.** When Socrates stood trial, he acted as his own lawyer.

_____ **4.** Socrates was Plato's teacher.

_____ **5.** Socrates died of old age.

**B. Following are some ideas of famous Athenian thinkers. Choose *one* and write a paragraph telling how you could apply the philosophy to your own life. Write your paragraph on a separate sheet of paper.**

Socrates: "Know thyself!"

Plato: "Wrong-doing is caused by ignorance; goodness is based on knowledge."

Aristotle: "Let us first know more of life. . . ."

© Pearson Education, Inc., publishing as Globe Fearon. All rights reserved.

**8 ▶ Identifying Fact and Opinion** **Exercise 21**

**A. Decide whether each statement is a fact or an opinion. Write *F* for *Fact* or *O* for *Opinion* on the line. Remember that a fact can be proven. An opinion is what someone believes.**

_____ **1.** Alexander the Great was brave, brilliant, and ambitious.

_____ **2.** Alexander the Great conquered the Phoenician city of Tyre.

_____ **3.** Alexander's teacher was Aristotle.

_____ **4.** Alexander made Ptolemy the ruler of Egypt.

_____ **5.** Alexander conquered the Indus River Valley, but went no farther into India.

_____ **6.** Alexandria was a magnificent city.

_____ **7.** Alexandria is in Egypt.

_____ **8.** The library in Alexandria contained more than 700,000 scrolls.

_____ **9.** If Alexander had not died at such an early age, he would probably have conquered the whole world.

_____ **10.** Alexander died at age 33.

**B. Choose one of the people listed below. Review the information about the person in Chapter 8. Then find more information in an encyclopedia, in another reference book, or possibly on the Internet. Write two or three paragraphs summarizing the person's life and accomplishments.**

| | |
|---|---|
| Aristotle | King Darius III |
| King Philip II | Ptolemy |

© Pearson Education, Inc., publishing as Globe Fearon.
All rights reserved.

# 8 ▶ Predicting What Might Have Happened

**Exercise 22**

*Critical Thinking*

**Write a brief paragraph to answer each question.**

**1.** After conquering the Indus River Valley, Alexander wanted to continue his campaign through India. His tired soldiers refused to continue. What do you think would have happened if Alexander's armies had agreed to continue the campaign through India?

_____

_____

_____

_____

_____

**2.** Alexander was a better warrior than ruler. After conquering lands, he usually turned them over to a chosen ruler. Because of this, he had trouble keeping control of his entire empire. What do you think would have happened if Alexander had been as interested in ruling as he was in conquering?

_____

_____

_____

_____

_____

**3.** When Alexander died at age 33, his lands were divided among some of his generals. The great empire was gone, split into separate smaller empires. What do you think would have happened if Alexander had not died at such a young age?

_____

_____

_____

_____

_____

© Pearson Education, Inc., publishing as Globe Fearon. All rights reserved.

Name _____   Date _____

## 9 ▶ Completing an Outline                                 **Exercise 23**

**Write each of the following sentences under the correct topic in the outline.**

- The Romans persecuted Christians for 300 years.
- The Roman Republic was divided into provinces, each ruled by its own governor.
- In A.D. 313, the Emperor Constantine made Christianity legal.
- The Roman Republic had a democratic form of government.
- Romans once believed in gods and goddesses similar to those the Greeks worshiped.
- The Romans built huge public baths that became the center of social life.
- In the Roman Republic, representatives elected by the people met in a senate.
- Romans, both rich and poor, attended chariot races for entertainment.
- Octavian became the Emperor Augustus, Rome's first emperor.
- The Emperor Augustus chose all the senators himself.
- Gladiator fights in the Roman amphitheater provided a violent form of sport.
- A fine system of highways linked the Roman provinces.

**I. Roman Politics**

    a. _____

    b. _____

    c. _____

    d. _____

    e. _____

**II. Roman Life**

    a. _____

    b. _____

    c. _____

    d. _____

**III. Roman Religion**

    a. _____

    b. _____

    c. _____

© Pearson Education, Inc., publishing as Globe Fearon. All rights reserved.

# 9 ▶ Classifying Terms/Debating an Issue

**Exercise 24**

*Critical Thinking*

**A. Circle the item in each group that does *not* belong.**

1. Roman emperors

   Nero      Augustus      Paul      Constantine

2. Romance languages

   Italian      French      Spanish      Arabic      Portuguese

3. Those who plotted to kill Caesar

   Cleopatra      Brutus      Cassius

4. Reasons Rome fell

   changes in climate      invaders from the north      high taxes      unemployment

5. Different names for the city where Constantine set up his capital

   Byzantium      Constantinople      Istanbul      Carthage

**B. Some Romans felt that Caesar had to die. Others supported him. Brutus was Caesar's friend, yet Brutus believed that Caesar must be killed. Write a paragraph explaining why Brutus plotted to assassinate Caesar.**

**Mark Antony remained loyal to Caesar. Write a paragraph explaining why he supported Caesar.**

**Write your two paragraphs on a separate sheet of paper.**

© Pearson Education, Inc., publishing as Globe Fearon. All rights reserved.

# 9 ▸ Using a Code

**Exercise 25**

*Critical Thinking*

**A.** When you fill in the blanks below with the correct words from the list, you will discover a code. Each number represents the letter above it. Use the code to find the answer to the question at the bottom of the page.

*republic     senator     forum     crucifixion     gladiator     pope*

**1.** a lawmaker

$\overline{1}$  $\overline{12}$  $\overline{15}$  $\overline{4}$  $\overline{30}$  $\overline{18}$  $\overline{5}$

**2.** a Roman public square where lawmakers met

$\overline{9}$  $\overline{18}$  $\overline{5}$  $\overline{7}$  $\overline{34}$

**3.** a democratic government; citizens elect representatives to make their laws

$\overline{5}$  $\overline{12}$  $\overline{21}$  $\overline{7}$  $\overline{40}$  $\overline{3}$  $\overline{6}$  $\overline{2}$

**4.** the head of the Roman Catholic Church

$\overline{21}$  $\overline{18}$  $\overline{21}$  $\overline{12}$

**5.** one who fought in the arenas of ancient Rome

$\overline{19}$  $\overline{3}$  $\overline{4}$  $\overline{8}$  $\overline{6}$  $\overline{4}$  $\overline{30}$  $\overline{18}$  $\overline{5}$

**6.** the putting to death of someone by nailing or tying that person to a cross

$\overline{2}$  $\overline{5}$  $\overline{7}$  $\overline{2}$  $\overline{6}$  $\overline{9}$  $\overline{6}$  $\overline{20}$  $\overline{6}$  $\overline{18}$  $\overline{15}$

**B.** Use the code to answer this question.

The Emperor Augustus brought a time of peace and prosperity to Rome. What was this time called?

$\overline{21}$  $\overline{4}$  $\overline{20}$    $\overline{5}$  $\overline{18}$  $\overline{34}$  $\overline{4}$  $\overline{15}$  $\overline{4}$

© Pearson Education, Inc., publishing as Globe Fearon.
All rights reserved.

Name _____   Date _____

# 10 ▶ Putting Events in Order                                   Exercise 26

*Skill Practice*

**Write the date of each event on the lines below. Then write the events in the order in which they occurred. Refer to Chapter 10 and to the timeline at the end of the chapter if you need help.**

(a) William conquers England in the Battle of Hastings in the year _____.

(b) The Vandals attack Rome in the year _____.

(c) Vikings begin raids on Europe in the year _____.

(d) The Goths enter Rome in the year _____.

(e) Charlemagne is crowned Holy Roman Emperor in the year _____.

(f) German chief Odoacer overthrows last of Roman Emperors in the year _____.

(g) Christian Church splits into Roman Catholic and Eastern Orthodox in the year

_____.

1. _____

2. _____

3. _____

4. _____

5. _____

6. _____

7. _____

© Pearson Education, Inc., publishing as Globe Fearon. All rights reserved.

# 10 ▸ Identifying and Understanding Point of View    **Exercise 27**

**A.** Different people look at situations and events differently. The way they see things may depend on their past experiences, where they live, and what they have been taught to believe. The way people look at things is called *point of view.* For example, the Goths must have considered Alaric a hero. The Romans certainly saw him as a villain.

Each of the following statements would have most likely come from a certain group of people. Which group of people would have said each of the following? Write the correct group from the list on the line.

*Romans     Goths     Franks     English     Vikings*

_____ **1.** "We shall follow Alaric into Rome!"

_____ **2.** "Hail Charlemagne, our mighty king!"

_____ **3.** "Lord, deliver us from the fury of the Northmen!"

_____ **4.** "Those uncivilized northerners are barbarians!"

_____ **5.** "We shall sail. We shall explore. We shall fight. And when we are done, Valhalla awaits us where we shall feast with the gods!"

**B.** Show that you understand the concept of point of view by completing the following assignment. Write a paragraph describing what it would be like to settle in a new land from the point of view of a Viking. Where did you settle? What is the land like? Do you like being in a new home? Then write a second paragraph describing Vikings settling in your country from the point of view of an English person. What do you think of these new people? What are they like? Write your paragraphs on a separate sheet of paper.

© Pearson Education, Inc., publishing as Globe Fearon.
All rights reserved.

# 10 ▶ Using a Chart

**A.** Use the information in the chart below to answer each item.

| The Major Gods and Goddesses of Norse Mythology | |
| --- | --- |
| **Name** | **Description** |
| Odin | chief of the gods |
| Frigga | mother of the gods, wife of Odin |
| Thor | god of thunder, son of Odin |
| Balder | god of sunlight, son of Odin |
| Hoder | god of winter, blind son of Odin |
| Sif | wife of Thor |
| Loki | god of fire, mischief-making god |
| Freya | goddess of love and beauty |
| Iduna | goddess of youth |
| Hermod | messenger of the gods |
| Hel | goddess of death, queen of the underworld |

1. The Norse god who was most likely to make trouble was named _____.

2. The Norsemen thought a clap of thunder came from the god named

   _____.

3. _____ was the chief of the Norse gods.

**B.** You will find similarities between the Greek gods and goddesses and the Norse deities. Compare the different cultures by filling in the lines.

1. The Greeks called the queen of their gods Hera. The Norse called her

   _____.

2. The Greeks called their goddess of love and beauty Aphrodite. The Norse called

   her _____.

3. Hermes was the Greek messenger of the gods. The Norse messenger-god was

   called _____

© Pearson Education, Inc., publishing as Globe Fearon. All rights reserved.

# 11 ▶ Identifying the Characteristics of a Society    Exercise 29

Chapter 11 describes the characteristics of a feudal society. Decide if
each of the following statements describes a feudal society or a
nonfeudal society. Write *F* before the number of each statement that
describes a feudal society. Write *NF* before the number of each
statement that describes a nonfeudal society. You may review Chapter
11 of your textbook if you need help.

_____ **1.** A king rules the whole country and divides his lands among his nobles.

_____ **2.** The nobles pay homage to their king and are loyal to him.

_____ **3.** Serfs work for the lord of the manor, farming his land.

_____ **4.** Everyone has a voice in a democratic form of government.

_____ **5.** Workers are well paid for their services.

_____ **6.** Each class owes loyalty and service to the class above it.

_____ **7.** It is a classless society, based upon the idea that all people are equal.

_____ **8.** Plentiful trade between nations creates a rich exchange of ideas.

_____ **9.** Each village is self-sufficient, meeting all its own needs.

_____ **10.** Fine schools ensure that both the rich and the poor are well educated.

_____ **11.** Strict laws guarantee human rights for all people.

_____ **12.** Every important man is also a warrior.

© Pearson Education, Inc., publishing as Globe Fearon.
All rights reserved.

# 11 ▶ Supporting Your Opinion with Facts

**Exercise 30**

*Critical Thinking*

**A.** Write a paragraph telling how you feel about feudalism as a way to organize society. Your first sentence, or topic sentence, should state your opinion of the feudal system. Your paragraph should contain at least three facts that support your opinion.

_____

_____

_____

_____

_____

_____

_____

_____

_____

_____

_____

_____

_____

_____

**B.** Suppose you lived in a medieval village. You might be asked to draw a poster warning your fellow citizens to beware of the Black Death or advertising a coming event. You might announce a tournament among local knights. You might advertise a village fair. Draw your poster on a separate sheet of paper.

© Pearson Education, Inc., publishing as Globe Fearon. All rights reserved.

# 11 Writing a Diary Entry

**Exercise 31**

*Critical Thinking*

In Chapter 11, you read about the ways of life of different people in medieval Europe. You read about nobles or vassals. You read about freemen and serfs. You also read about the clergy and about pages, squires, and knights. Put yourself in the place of one of these people. Write a diary entry telling about a typical day in your life. Describe yourself. Include your likes and dislikes, your responsibilities, and your surroundings.

Date _____

Dear Diary,

_____

_____

_____

_____

_____

_____

_____

_____

_____

_____

_____

_____

_____

_____

_____

© Pearson Education, Inc., publishing as Globe Fearon. All rights reserved.

Name _____  Date _____

## 12 ▶ Using a Chart                                    Exercise 32
*Skill Practice*

Use the information in the chart below to answer the questions.

| Years | Military Events | Results |
|---|---|---|
| **First:** 1096–1099 | 1098–Antioch captured. | At least 35,000 people participated. |
| | 1099–Jerusalem fell to Christians. | 10,000 Jews and Muslims killed. |
| **Second:** 1144–1149 | 1144–City of Edessa lost to Turks. | Crusaders met defeat and failed to reach Jerusalem. |
| **Third:** 1187–1192 | 1187–Fall of Jerusalem to Muslim leader, Saladin. | Christians failed to take back Jerusalem. |
| **Fourth:** 1202–1204 | 1204–Capture of Constantinople; creation of Roman Christian Empire there until 1261. | Conditions in Holy Lands did not change; Muslims continued to rule. |
| **Later Crusades:** 1228–1270 | Christians secured Jerusalem by truce. | Muslims captured Jerusalem again in 1244. |
| | 1268–Antioch fell to Muslims. | No movement toward freeing the Holy Land. |
| 1291 | Muslims captured city of Acre. | Last Christian stronghold was taken by Muslims. |

1. In what year did Jerusalem first fall to the Christians? _____

2. When did the Muslim leader Saladin regain Jerusalem? _____

3. The Christians captured Constantinople in 1204. Who controlled the Holy Lands at that time? _____

4. The Christians captured the city of Antioch in 1098. When did the Muslims regain control of Antioch? _____

5. When did the last Christian stronghold in the Holy Lands fall to the Muslims? _____

© Pearson Education, Inc., publishing as Globe Fearon. All rights reserved.

Name_____  Date_____

A. Use the information in the chart below to answer the statements.

| Results of the Magna Carta | |
|---|---|
| **The Magna Carta———————→** | **Led to** |
| guaranteed that justice should not be sold or denied to freemen———————→ | *writ of habeas corpus* (a person can not be held in prison unless he or she has been formally charged with or convicted of a crime) |
| provided that taxes be collected by legal means, not by force———————→ | no taxation without representation |
| stated that no man might be imprisoned or his property taken from him except by fair and legal trial———→ | modern system of trial by a jury of equals |

1. The Magna Carta stated that justice could not be denied to _____.

2. Today's Americans cannot be held in prison unless they have been formally charged with or convicted of a crime. This is called a writ of _____.

3. According to the Magna Carta, a man could not be put in prison or his property taken from him until he had been _____.

B. Ideas based on the Magna Carta affected the writers of the U.S. Declaration of Independence and the Constitution. Write a paragraph explaining how you benefit from rights that can be traced back to the Magna Carta. Write your paragraph on a separate sheet of paper.

© Pearson Education, Inc., publishing as Globe Fearon. All rights reserved.

# 12 ▶ Using a Chart                                          Exercise 34

By the end of Chapter 12, your textbook has discussed the birth of several major religions. By looking at the chart below, you can make quick comparisons between four of the world's major religions. Use the information in the chart below to answer the questions.

|  | Christianity | Islam | Buddhism | Judaism |
|---|---|---|---|---|
| **Religious Figure** | Jesus Christ | Muhammad | Gautama Buddha | "Messiah" yet to come |
| **After Death** | afterlife | afterlife | reincarnation | afterlife |
| **Rewards for Good Deeds** | heaven | paradise | nirvana | heaven |
| **Holy Book** | Bible | Koran | the Tripitaka and Sutras (Buddha's teachings) | Jewish Bible (Tenach), includes Torah |
| **Place of Worship** | church, cathedral | mosque | temple | synagogue |
| **Number of Members Today (approximately)** | 1,974,181,000 | 1,155,109,000 | 356,270,000 | 14,313,000 |

1. Which religion has the most followers in the world? _____

2. Do all the religions listed on the chart promise people a reward for good deeds?

   _____

3. Which religion promises something other than an afterlife in heaven or paradise?

   _____

4. In which religion do the followers believe that their prophet or great religious teacher

   has not yet come to earth? _____

5. Where do followers of Muhammad go to worship? _____

© Pearson Education, Inc., publishing as Globe Fearon. All rights reserved.

Name_____     Date_____

Use the map to decide if the following statements are true or false. If
it is true, write *T.* If it is false, write *F.*

**The Spread of the Renaissance in Europe**

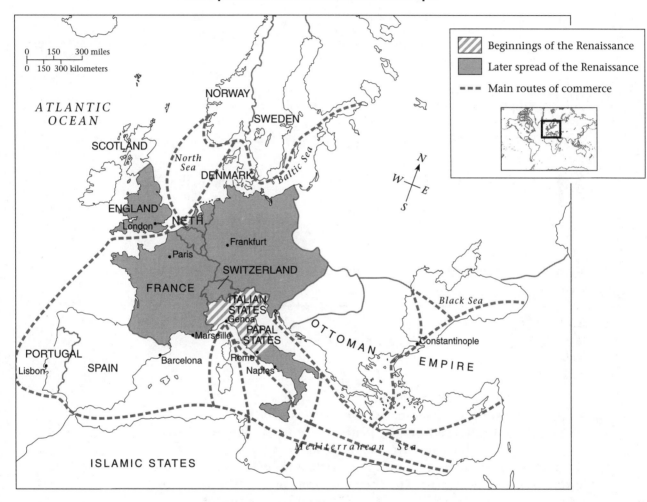

© Pearson Education, Inc., publishing as Globe Fearon.
All rights reserved.

_____ **1.** The Renaissance started in the cities of northern Italy.

_____ **2.** The Renaissance started in Spain.

_____ **3.** The Renaissance spread to Norway and Sweden.

_____ **4.** The Renaissance spread to England and France.

_____ **5.** The Renaissance spread to every nation that traded with Italy.

_____ **6.** The city of Constantinople was at the heart of the Renaissance.

_____ **7.** The Renaissance spread to Switzerland and the Netherlands.

# 13 ▸ Understanding Point of View

**Exercise 36**

*Critical Thinking*

**A.** Look at the two columns comparing the point of view of Medieval and Renaissance societies. Then answer the questions that follow.

| Medieval Point of View | Renaissance Point of View |
| --- | --- |
| Life after death is most important. | This life is important. |
| People can do nothing on their own. | People have ability and can achieve. |
| People are basically wicked. | People are good. |

**1.** Which point of view would place more emphasis on heaven and hell?

_____

**2.** Which point of view would lead people to build schools for increasing numbers of students?

_____

**3.** Which point of view would lead to new inventions and discoveries?

_____

**4.** Which point of view is closest to your own?

_____

**B.** Get into the spirit of the Renaissance. On a separate sheet of paper, create a project that reflects the Renaissance point of view. You might draw or paint a picture, make a collage, write a poem, describe or diagram an invention, or write a report about a modern accomplishment. The theme of your project should be one of the statements listed above under "Renaissance Point of View":

**This life is important.**

**People have ability and can achieve.**

**People are good.**

© Pearson Education, Inc., publishing as Globe Fearon. All rights reserved.

# 13 ▶ Classifying Religious Movements         Exercise 37

**A.** The Reformation was a religious movement of the 1500s. It was a
reaction against the power of the Roman Catholic Church. The
Counter Reformation was a movement for change within the
Roman Catholic Church itself.

    Each of the following items relates either to the Reformation
or the Counter Reformation. List each item in its proper category.
Use information from Chapter 13 to help you classify the items.

| Martin Luther | St. Ignatius Loyola | 95 complaints | John Calvin |
| Huguenots | Protestantism | Jesuits | |

**Reformation**                         **Counter Reformation**

_____          _____

_____          _____

_____          _____

_____          _____

_____          _____

**B.** The Roman Catholic Church succeeded in preventing revolt in
Spain, Italy, and some other countries. However, Protestantism
became the chief religion of the countries of northwestern Europe.
An almanac will provide information about the major religions of
different countries today. Use a recent almanac to find out if the
results of the Reformation are reflected today. The first item has
been done for you as an example.

| Country | Major religion | Country | Major religion |
|---|---|---|---|
| Spain | *Roman Catholic* | Poland | _____ |
| Italy | _____ | Sweden | _____ |
| Hungary | _____ | Denmark | _____ |
| Norway | _____ | Finland | _____ |

© Pearson Education, Inc., publishing as Globe Fearon. All rights reserved.

# 14 ▶ Writing About Monarchs

Choose *Assignment A* or *Assignment B*. (Continue writing on a separate sheet of paper if you need more room.)

**A.** Write a conversation that might have taken place between one of the following pairs.

King Philip II of Spain and Queen Mary I of England

King Philip II of Spain and William of Orange of the Netherlands

King Henry VIII of England and Anne Boleyn

**B.** You are a reporter interviewing one of the monarchs described in Chapter 14. Write five questions that you would ask the person. Write five answers that you suppose he or she might give in response.

_____

_____

_____

_____

_____

_____

_____

_____

_____

_____

_____

_____

_____

© Pearson Education, Inc., publishing as Globe Fearon. All rights reserved.

# 14 ▶ Matching People, Items, and Events     Exercise 39

**A.** Match the names of the rulers listed on the left with their descriptions listed on the right. Write the correct letter on the line before the ruler's name.

_____ **1.** King Philip II of Spain          **a.** six wives

_____ **2.** King Henry IV of France       **b.** nicknamed the "Bloody" queen

_____ **3.** King Henry VIII of England   **c.** nicknamed the "Good Queen Bess"

_____ **4.** Queen Mary I of England      **d.** the Edict of Nantes

_____ **5.** Queen Elizabeth I of England  **e.** the throne at age 9

_____ **6.** King Edward VI of England    **f.** the Spanish Armada

**B.** Look at each quote below. Choose from the list above to name the monarch who most likely would have said the words.

**1.** "The people of the Netherlands will accept the Catholic religion!"

_____

**2.** "My husband and I shall fight together under the sign of the cross. We shall crush Protestantism and see all of Europe under the Catholic Church."

_____

**3.** "I must become a Catholic to bring peace to my country. But I shall insist on religious freedom for my people."

_____

**4.** "If she cannot give me a son, I say 'off with her head!'"

_____

© Pearson Education, Inc., publishing as Globe Fearon. All rights reserved.

# 15 ▸ Writing a Poem

The feudal society in Europe was a military one, and a man's success depended on his strength and military skill. Much of the arts were related to the church. In feudal Europe, little importance was placed on education or on the arts outside the church. This did not happen in feudal Japan. Although strength and military skill were important, scholars continued to be admired. In contrast to Europe, the arts flourished in feudal Japan.

The Japanese believed everyone could take part in the enjoyment and creation of art, literature, and music. Ordinary people often made up short poems to describe a lovely scene or a special occasion. They even held contests and games in which people made up short poems called *haiku*. A haiku is a poem containing 17 syllables—5 in the first line, 7 in the second, and 5 in the third. It captures a single moment. It may be sad, happy, or thoughtful.

**Read the following haiku. Then try to create your own version of this ancient Japanese form of verse.**

*Eaten by the cat!*
*Perhaps the cricket's widow*
*Is bewailing that.*

*The summer grasses*
*Wave like a warrior's arms,*
*Wave in the red sun.*

*Fish hide in shadows,*
*Darkened corners of the pool*
*Offer cool and peace.*

**Write a haiku of your own. Look around you for your subject matter. Your dog, a tree outside the window, a baseball field—anything will do. Write your haiku on the lines below. If you have time, write others on a separate sheet of paper.**

_____

_____

_____

© Pearson Education, Inc., publishing as Globe Fearon. All rights reserved.

# 15 ▷ Grouping Information

**Write each of the following sentences under the correct category in the outline.**

The Silk Road provides a link to the Western world.

Samurai warriors fight for the nobles in return for wealth and land.

The Ganges River is considered holy.

Emperors live in the Forbidden City.

The shogun is the real ruler.

Marco Polo calls this land *Cipango,* land of gold and riches.

The Mogul Empire lasts for 200 years.

Mongols rule this nation from 1260 until 1368.

Isolation turns this country into a hermit nation.

   **I. China**

      a. _____

      b. _____

      c. _____

   **II. Japan**

      a. _____

      b. _____

      c. _____

      d. _____

   **III. India**

      a. _____

      b. _____

© Pearson Education, Inc., publishing as Globe Fearon.
All rights reserved.

## 16 ▶ Predicting What Might Have Happened    Exercise 42

**Write a brief paragraph to answer each question.**

1. Christopher Columbus planned to find a short sea route to India. He wanted three ships, a share of the trade, and the governorship of any lands he explored. He wanted the title of admiral and a noble rank. In 1482, Columbus presented his plan to the king of Portugal. The king refused Columbus's request. Columbus finally convinced Queen Isabella of Spain to support his voyage. It was on this voyage that Columbus landed in the Americas. He claimed the land in the name of Spain. How do you think history would have developed if the king of Portugal had supported Columbus's voyage?

_____

_____

_____

_____

_____

_____

2. Hernando Cortéz conquered the Aztecs of Mexico in 1521. Francisco Pizaro conquered the Incas of Peru in 1532. Both Cortéz and Pizaro treated the native people cruelly, cheating them and using them as slaves. What do you think would have happened if the Spanish conquerors had respected the Native Americans and treated them fairly? What might be different today?

_____

_____

_____

_____

_____

_____

© Pearson Education, Inc., publishing as Globe Fearon. All rights reserved.

Name _____   Date _____

Use the information in the map below to choose the one best answer
to each item. (You may want to look at a modern world map to
identify current place names.)

**European Conquest and Colonization, About 1750**

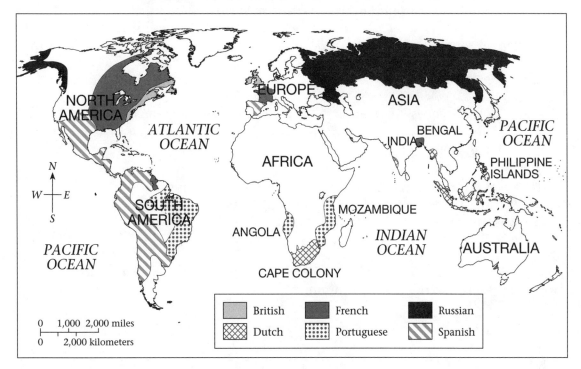

1. In 1750, land that is part of Alaska today belonged to

   **(a)** Britain.      **(b)** Russia.      **(c)** France.

2. Land that is called Mexico today belonged to

   **(a)** Spain.      **(b)** Portugal.      **(c)** France.

3. Parts of Africa were colonized by the

   **(a)** Russians and Spaniards.      **(b)** French and Dutch.      **(c)** Dutch and Portuguese.

4. South America had settlements controlled by the

   **(a)** Portuguese, Spanish,      **(b)** Portuguese, Spanish,      **(c)** British, French,
   and British.                          and Dutch.                          and Spanish.

5. Land that is part of Canada today was settled by colonists from

   **(a)** Britain and France.      **(b)** Spain and Portugal.      **(c)** Russia and France.

© Pearson Education, Inc., publishing as Globe Fearon.
All rights reserved.

# 17 ▶ Classifying Historical Figures

**Exercise 44**

**A.** Each of the following historical figures is discussed in Chapter 17. Some of them stood on the side of democracy and new freedoms. Others supported the rights of monarchs to rule with absolute power and fought the rising tide of democracy. Write *D* before the number of those who supported moves toward democracy. Write *M* before the number of those who supported the absolute power of monarchs.

_____ **1.** John Locke                 _____ **5.** King Charles I

_____ **2.** Voltaire                    _____ **6.** William and Mary

_____ **3.** Jean Jacques Rousseau       _____ **7.** Thomas Jefferson

_____ **4.** King Edward I

**B.** Voltaire was a famous French writer and philosopher during the Age of Reason. In his writings, he attacked religious and political tyranny. Write a paragraph explaining what Voltaire meant when he wrote:

"It is forbidden to kill. Therefore all murderers are punished unless they kill in large numbers and to the sound of trumpets."

_____

_____

_____

_____

_____

_____

_____

_____

_____

_____

_____

© Pearson Education, Inc., publishing as Globe Fearon. All rights reserved.

# 17 ▸ Understanding the Bill of Rights

**Exercise 45**

*Critical Thinking*

**A.** Most democratic countries have a bill of rights as a part of their constitution. It guarantees certain rights to the citizens. You can read about the English Bill of Rights in Chapter 17 of your textbook.

    In 1791, the American Bill of Rights was added to the U. S. Constitution. It was made up of ten amendments that promised citizens certain freedoms. Look up the Bill of Rights in an almanac or an encyclopedia. List five freedoms that the Bill of Rights guarantees.

   **1.** _____

   **2.** _____

   **3.** _____

   **4.** _____

   **5.** _____

**B.** Suppose you have the chance to create your own personal bill of rights. Perhaps your list of rights will be honored by your school or your family or your boss. List five rights you believe you would include in your bill of rights.

   **1.** _____

   **2.** _____

   **3.** _____

   **4.** _____

   **5.** _____

© Pearson Education, Inc., publishing as Globe Fearon. All rights reserved.

# 18 ▶ Solving a Crossword Puzzle

**Exercise 46**

*Review*

Use the clues below to solve the puzzle about the French Revolution.

**ACROSS**

1. King Louis' number

4. An attack on this French prison began the French Revolution.

5. cry heard during the Reign of Terror: "Off with their_____!"

7. the group that wrote the new French Constitution

8. a governing body: the "_____ General"

12. a violent leader of the French Revolution

14. This machine quickly cuts off heads!

**DOWN**

2. a fine palace outside of Paris

3. a Frenchman who helped the American colonists battle the British

6. the site of a meeting of rebels

9. the peasants and working-class French were represented by this estate

10. motto of the French Republic: "_____, Equality, and Fraternity!"

11. The French Bill of Rights: The Declaration of the Rights of

_____

13. All the French celebrate Bastille Day during this month.

© Pearson Education, Inc., publishing as Globe Fearon. All rights reserved.

# 18 ▶ Putting Events in Order                    Exercise 47

The following events mark the rise and fall of Napoleon Bonaparte.
They are not listed in the order in which they occurred. Write the year
of each event on the line provided. Then on the lines below, write the
events in the order in which they actually occurred. Review Chapter
18 and the timeline at the end of that chapter if you need help.

**1.** Napoleon declares war on Russia in the year _____.

**2.** Napoleon meets defeat at Waterloo in the year _____.

**3.** Napoleon pushes out the Directory and becomes dictator of France in the year

_____.

**4.** Napoleon dies in exile on the island of Saint Helena in the year _____.

**5.** Napoleon has himself crowned emperor of France in the year _____.

**6.** Louis XVIII takes the throne from Napoleon, and Napoleon is exiled in the year

_____.

**1.** _____

_____

**2.** _____

_____

**3.** _____

_____

**4.** _____

_____

**5.** _____

_____

**6.** _____

_____

© Pearson Education, Inc., publishing as Globe Fearon.
All rights reserved.

# 18 ▶ Identifying Causes and Results

**Exercise 48**

**A.** Some of the following items describe *causes* of the French
   Revolution. Other items describe *results* of the French Revolution.
   Write a *C* before the items that describe causes of the Revolution.
   Write an *R* before items that describe its results.

_____ **1.** French nobles lived in high style, while peasants often went without
   enough to eat.

_____ **2.** The king was out of money and wanted higher taxes.

_____ **3.** Though it represented 98 percent of the people, the Third Estate had
   only one vote.

_____ **4.** Nobles lost their feudal rights, and the king lost much of his power.

_____ **5.** Writers like Rousseau and Voltaire spoke of freedom and human rights.

_____ **6.** The National Assembly issued the Declaration of the Rights of Man.

_____ **7.** France was declared a republic.

_____ **8.** The American Revolution provided an example of a successful fight
   for freedom.

**B.** Some people might say that Napoleon Bonaparte was good for
   France. Others would say that his intentions and his actions were
   bad. Points can be made on both sides of this issue. In the *positive*
   column, list the good contributions that Napoleon made. In the
   *negative* column, list his negative points.

| Positive | Negative |
|---|---|
| _____ | _____ |
| _____ | _____ |
| _____ | _____ |
| _____ | _____ |
| _____ | _____ |
| _____ | _____ |
| _____ | _____ |

© Pearson Education, Inc., publishing as Globe Fearon.
All rights reserved.

# 19 ▶ Completing a Chart

The chart below lists machines invented during the Industrial Revolution. Complete the chart by filling in the blank spaces with either the name of the invention, the year of the invention, the name of the inventor, or the inventor's nationality. You may review Chapter 19 of your textbook if you need help.

| Inventions that Changed the World | | | |
|---|---|---|---|
| **Invention** | **Date** | **Inventor** | **Nationality** |
| First commercial steam engine | 1698 | **1.** _____ | British |
| Flying shuttle | 1733 | John Kay | **2.** _____ |
| Spinning jenny | **3.** _____ | James Hargreaves | British |
| Water frame | 1769 | **4.** _____ | British |
| Improved steam engine | **5.** _____ | James Watt | Scottish |
| Mule | 1779 | **6.** _____ | British |
| Steam-powered loom | **7.** _____ | Edmund Cartwright | British |
| First steam locomotive | **8.** _____ | Richard Trevithick | British |
| **9.** _____ | 1807 | Robert Fulton | American |
| Dynamo | 1831 | **10.** _____ | British |

© Pearson Education, Inc., publishing as Globe Fearon. All rights reserved.

**19** ▶ **Understanding a Pie Graph**                    **Exercise 50**

Study the pie graphs below. Then answer the questions on the lines below.

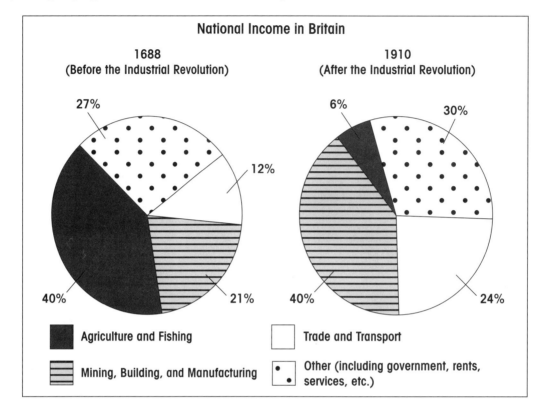

**National Income in Britain**

**1688**
(Before the Industrial Revolution)

**1910**
(After the Industrial Revolution)

■ Agriculture and Fishing        □ Trade and Transport

▤ Mining, Building, and Manufacturing    ⊡ Other (including government, rents, services, etc.)

1. Which economic activities produced the most income in 1688?

   _____

2. Which produced the most income in 1910?

   _____

3. Which decreased the most between 1688 and 1910?

   _____

4. Which economic activities about doubled between 1688 and 1910?

   _____

5. How did the Industrial Revolution affect agriculture in Britain?

   _____

© Pearson Education, Inc., publishing as Globe Fearon. All rights reserved.

# 19 ▶ Thinking About Industrialization Today         Exercise 51

**A.** Chapter 19 describes the Industrial Revolution of the 1700s and 1800s. There have been other industrial revolutions around the world. Some nations are growing industrially today, whereas others continue to depend on agriculture.

   The list below shows the percentage of the labor force working in industry as compared to agriculture in several nations. If more of the labor force is involved in industry, write *I* before the number. If more of the labor force is involved in agriculture, write *A* before the number.

_____ **1.** Haiti: industry = 9%; agriculture = 66%

_____ **2.** France: industry = 26%; agriculture = 5%

_____ **3.** Germany: industry = 34%; agriculture = 3%

_____ **4.** Nigeria: industry = 6%; agriculture = 54%

_____ **5.** Ecuador: industry = 35%; agriculture = 30%

_____ **6.** Sudan: industry = 10%; agriculture = 80%

_____ **7.** India: industry = 15%; agriculture = 67%

_____ **8.** China: industry = 24%; agriculture = 50%

_____ **9.** Norway: industry = 22%; agriculture = 4%

_____ **10.** Italy: industry = 32%; agriculture = 7%

_____ **11.** Mexico: industry = 21%; agriculture = 24%

**B.** Use the information in the list above to answer the questions. Then circle the one best answer.

   **1.** Which of the following European countries is the most industrialized?

   **a.** France     **b.** Germany     **c.** Italy

   **2.** In which country do almost the same number of people work in agriculture as in industry?

   **a.** Italy     **b.** India     **c.** Mexico

   **3.** Which of the following Latin American countries is the most agricultural?

   **a.** Mexico     **b.** Haiti     **c.** Ecuador

© Pearson Education, Inc., publishing as Globe Fearon. All rights reserved.

## 20 ▶ Understanding Point of View                    Exercise 52

**If you lived in colonial Latin America, you would probably have a different point of view depending on your social class. Reread the section called *Social Classes in the Colonies* in Chapter 20. Then decide if each of the following statements represents the point of view of a *Spaniard,* a *Creole,* a *mestizo,* an *Indian,* or an *African slave.* Write the social class you choose on the line after the statement.**

1.  "We bring our culture, our knowledge, and our religion to this savage land. We will rule this land, and we will civilize its people."

    _____

2.  "My father came from across the sea. My mother is a native of this land. Though some people scorn me, I feel that I combine the best of two cultures. I will fight for freedom and respect!"

    _____

3.  "I am ready to stand up against the rulers of this land. They brought me here against my will. They made me work for them but gave me nothing in return. I know I shall never see my homeland again, so I am ready to fight to make my new land free!"

    _____

4.  "This is my land! My people lived here long before any others. Then conquerors came from beyond the sea. They seized the land and made my people work for them like animals. They took our gold and silver. We want our freedom once again."

    _____

5.  "I consider myself a Spanish American. My parents came from Spain, but I was born in this new land. I appreciate my Spanish heritage, but I believe the time has come to be free from ties with Spain!"

    _____

© Pearson Education, Inc., publishing as Globe Fearon. All rights reserved.

**20** **Word Play**

Circle the correct answer in each group of phrases. Then put the answers together, sound them out, and they will help you come up with a final answer. Write on the line. (The final answers are all mentioned in Chapter 20.)

**1.** the opposite of *she:*
he     her     boy

**2.** a child's toy:
cookie     doll     mother

**3.** the opposite of stay:
remain     go     sleep

   **Final answer**—This man fought for Mexico's independence:

   _____

**4.** the opposite of *order:*
mess     organization     delay

**5.** to make fun of:
praise     tease     applaud

**6.** an exclamation of surprise:
Good-bye!     Oh!     Alas!

   **Final answer**—a person of mixed race:

   _____

**7.** a laughing sound:
ouch!     ha!     ole!

**8.** another word for *ocean:*
river     plain     sea

**9.** the opposite of *beginning:*
start     end     middle

**10.** you and I together make:
them     me     us

   **Final answer**—large Spanish-style ranches:

   _____

**11.** a synonym for *automobile:*
car     train     plane

**12.** a bone in your chest:
spine     skull     rib

**13.** Lima, string, kidney, pinto, and navy are all a kind of:
bean     river     automobile

   **Final answer**—a sea surrounding the island of Haiti:

   _____

© Pearson Education, Inc., publishing as Globe Fearon. All rights reserved.

Name _____     Date _____

Use the information in the map below to answer the questions.

**The United States Expands Westward**

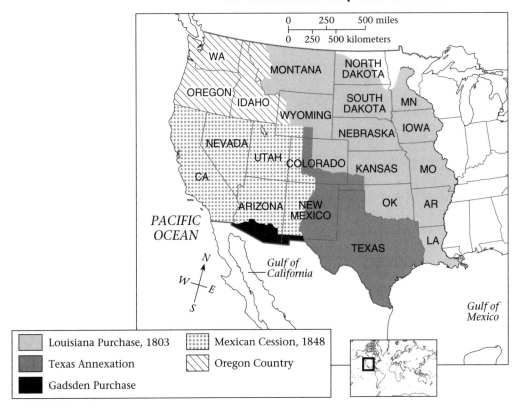

1. **The Gadsden Purchase was named after the U.S. agent who arranged to buy the land from Mexico. The Gadsden Purchase included lands that are today part of**

   what two states? _____ and _____

2. **When was the Mexican Cession added?** _____

3. **Which addition included lands that spanned the United States from its northern**

   border to its southern border? _____

4. **The Oregon Country included land that is today part of what five states?**

   _____, _____, _____,

   _____, and _____

5. **The state of California once belonged to what country?** _____

© Pearson Education, Inc., publishing as Globe Fearon. All rights reserved.

Name_____     Date_____

 **21** **Making Comparisons/Predicting Events**          **Exercise 55**

**A.** **Follow the directions for each numbered statement.**

**1.** During the 1800s, the United States established clear northern and southern borders. Compare the way the United States established its northern border with the way it established its southern border.

_____

_____

_____

_____

_____

**2.** Compare the results of the War of 1812 with the results of the Spanish-American War of 1898. Which war resulted in the United States gaining new lands? Which war resulted in no lands gained and no lands lost?

_____

_____

_____

_____

**B.** **Follow the directions for each numbered statement. Then write your answers on a separate sheet of paper.**

**1.** The United States government fought the Civil War to hold on to its own lands in the South. The South lost the war, and the United States remained one nation. What do you think would have happened if the South had won the Civil War?

**2.** Many Americans said that U.S. Secretary of State William Seward was a fool to buy Alaska from Russia. What do you think would have happened if Seward had listened to those people and had refused the purchase?

© Pearson Education, Inc., publishing as Globe Fearon. All rights reserved.

Name _____     Date _____

# 21 ▶ Using a Map

Study the map. Then follow the directions below. You will need
colored pens, pencils, or crayons to complete this exercise.

**The Panama Canal: 1914**

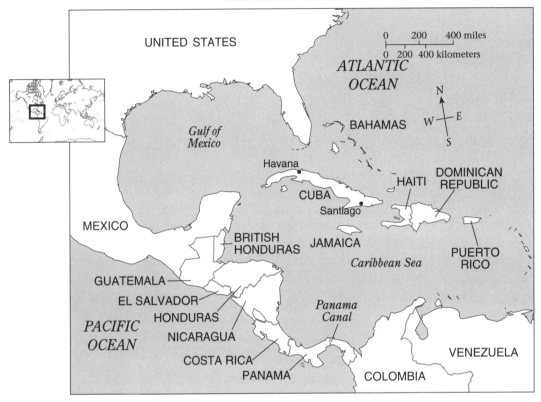

1. The Panama Canal was built by the United States. Circle the Panama Canal in *red*.

2. At the time U.S. President Theodore Roosevelt wanted to build a canal across
   Panama, Colombia ruled Panama. Color the country of Panama *yellow*. Color
   the country of Colombia *brown*.

3. The Panama Canal links the Pacific Ocean and the Caribbean Sea. Circle the
   words "Pacific Ocean" in *blue*. Circle the words "Caribbean Sea" in *green*.

4. Draw a *black* line showing the route a ship would take if it were traveling
   from the west coast of Guatemala to Havana, Cuba.

© Pearson Education, Inc., publishing as Globe Fearon.
All rights reserved.

# 22 ▶ Placing Events in Time

**Exercise 57**

*Skill Practice*

The following events *are not* listed in the order in which they occurred. Decide during which time period each event occurred. Write *A*, *B*, or *C* on each line. You may review Chapter 22 in your textbook if you need help.

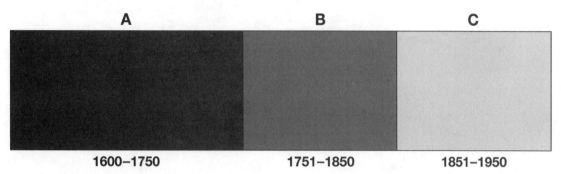

|  A  |  B  |  C  |
| :---: | :---: | :---: |
| 1600–1750 | 1751–1850 | 1851–1950 |

1. The Manchus invade China. _____

2. The Qing dynasty rules China. _____

3. China and Britain fight Opium War. _____

4. Chinese peasants revolt in Taiping Rebellion. _____

5. Boxer Rebellion attempts to keep all foreigners out of China. _____

6. Sun Yatsen leads rebellion and overthrows Manchus. _____

7. China and Japan go to war. _____

8. Japan wins war with China. _____

9. Japan is an isolated nation. _____

10. Commodore Perry first comes to Japan. _____

11. Japan signs trade treaty with United States. _____

12. Meiji period provides "enlightened rule" for Japan. _____

13. Japan wins war with Russia. _____

14. Japan takes over Korea. _____

15. Japan writes its first constitution. _____

© Pearson Education, Inc., publishing as Globe Fearon. All rights reserved.

Name _____     Date _____

Use the map below and information in Chapter 22 to answer the questions.

**Japan**

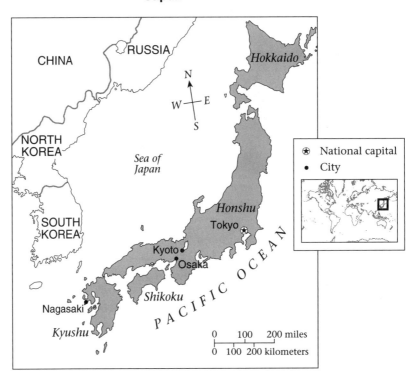

1.  The four main islands of Japan are labeled on the map. Name those four islands.

    _____, _____, _____, and

    _____.

2.  The Tokugawa shoguns set up their capital at what is now called Tokyo. On which

    island is the city of Tokyo? _____

3.  Japan was isolated under Tokugawa rule. No foreign ships were allowed to enter

    Japanese ports. Name three ports shown on this map. _____,

    _____, and _____

4.  From 1894 to 1895, Japan fought and won a war with one of the countries shown

    on this map. Name that country. _____

5.  Name a country that Japan took control of in 1910. _____

© Pearson Education, Inc., publishing as Globe Fearon. All rights reserved.

# 23 ▶ Identifying Point of View

**Exercise 59**

*Critical Thinking*

**A.** In 1858, the British took over direct rule of India. The British said that India profited from British control. Many Indians, however, saw things differently. Read each of the following statements. Identify the point of view as British or as Indian. Write *B* or *I* beside each number.

_____ **1.** India's wealth and raw materials are being used to help Great Britain, not India!

_____ **2.** We resent the fact that all of India's top jobs are going to foreigners!

_____ **3.** We build fine new schools, hospitals, railroads, and factories to make life better in India.

_____ **4.** We cannot eat in certain restaurants. We cannot sleep in certain hotels. Our society has become segregated.

_____ **5.** The caste system keeps many people poor. We must see that it is ended.

_____ **6.** Our native culture is being destroyed!

_____ **7.** All of the highest government positions are being filled by foreigners.

**B.** On a separate sheet of paper, write a short news story based on one of the following headlines.

**SOLDIERS REFUSE TO BITE THE BULLET**

**THOUSANDS JOIN MARCH TO THE SEA**

**INDIAN LEADER REFUSES TO EAT**

© Pearson Education, Inc., publishing as Globe Fearon. All rights reserved.

# 23 ▶ Making Comparisons                                    Exercise 60

**Write one or two paragraphs to complete each of the activities below.**

1. Compare British imperialism in India (Chapter 23) with Spanish imperialism in Latin America (Chapter 20). Discuss the ways the imperial powers gained rule as well as the attitudes of the imperial powers toward the native-born people. Compare the reactions of the native peoples to their rulers and the movements for independence.

   _____

   _____

   _____

   _____

   _____

   _____

   _____

2. Compare Mahatma Gandhi's ideas about rebellion and protest with those of U.S. civil rights leader Martin Luther King Jr. You can use an encyclopedia, another reference book, or possibly the Internet to learn more about these historical figures.

   _____

   _____

   _____

   _____

   _____

   _____

   _____

© Pearson Education, Inc., publishing as Globe Fearon. All rights reserved.

# 24 ▶ Comparing Civilizations

**Exercise 61**

*Review*

In Chapter 24, you read about the early civilizations of Africa. Each of the following descriptions applies to one of these civilizations. Beside each number, write *K* for the Kingdom of Kush, *G* for the Kingdom of Ghana, *M* for the Kingdom of Mali, or *S* for the Kingdom of Songhai. You may review the information, map, and timelines in Chapter 24 if you need help.

_____ **1.** This civilization began in about 2000 B.C. and lasted until about A.D. 350.

_____ **2.** This ancient kingdom of black Africans was also called Nubia.

_____ **3.** Mansa Musa ruled this kingdom and spread word of its gold and fabulous wealth.

_____ **4.** This kingdom was located just south of Egypt.

_____ **5.** This kingdom was at one time ruled by Egypt, but later it used iron weapons to conquer and rule Egypt.

_____ **6.** This kingdom took control in western Africa during the 1400s.

_____ **7.** Askia Mohammad ruled this kingdom from 1493 to 1528.

_____ **8.** The warriors fought Moroccan guns with their spears, and they lost their kingdom.

_____ **9.** This kingdom grew up in western Africa during the A.D. 400s and began to prosper about A.D. 1000.

_____ **10.** The Mandingo people took over this kingdom in the late 1200s.

© Pearson Education, Inc., publishing as Globe Fearon. All rights reserved.

## 24 ▶ Making a Graph/Stating Your Opinion          Exercise 62

*Skill Practice*

**A.** Make two pie graphs to represent the following information:

**African Territory**

**1876**

10.8%–controlled by European
    powers

89.2%–independent territory

**1900**

90.4%–controlled by European
    powers

9.6%–independent territory

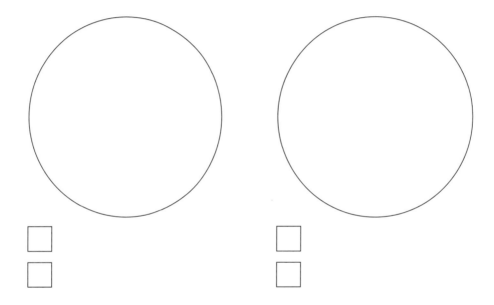

**B.** Write a paragraph to convince a reader that either slavery, racism,
or imperialism is wrong. Use examples from Chapter 24 to show
how slavery, racism, or imperialism hurt the people of Africa.
Write your paragraph on a separate sheet of paper.

© Pearson Education, Inc., publishing as Globe Fearon.
All rights reserved.

# 24 ▶ Using a Map

**Exercise 63**

*Skill Practice*

Use the informaton in the map below to answer the questions.

**European Colonies in Africa, 1920**

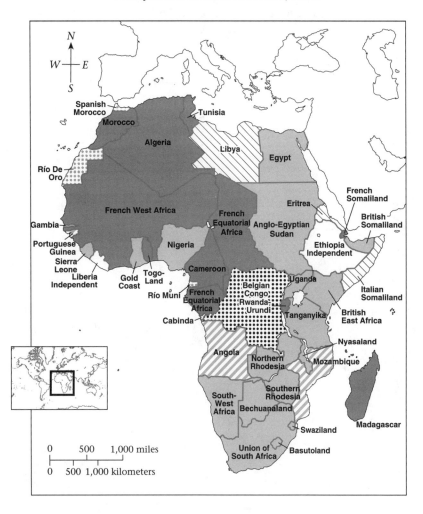

1. In 1920, which European nation controlled the Union of South Africa? _____

2. What two African nations were independent in 1920? _____

3. Which nation controlled Egypt in 1920? _____

4. Which nation controlled most of western Africa? _____

5. Which nation controlled the island of Madagascar? _____

6. Which two countries on the west coast of Africa were controlled by Portugal?

_____

© Pearson Education, Inc., publishing as Globe Fearon. All rights reserved.

## 25 ▶ Understanding Nationalism                          Exercise 64

*Critical Thinking*

**A.** Chapter 25 tells about nationalism, a feeling of pride in and loyalty toward one's country and culture. Nationalism leads people to honor their flag. Find the flag of Germany and of Italy in an almanac, or in an encyclopedia, or on the Internet. Sketch and color the flags in the spaces below.

**Italian Flag**

**German Flag**

**B.** In one or two paragraphs, describe an event during your own lifetime that encouraged U.S. nationalism and patriotism. Write your paragraphs on a separate sheet of paper.

© Pearson Education, Inc., publishing as Globe Fearon. All rights reserved.

Name _____     Date _____

Use the map below and information in Chapter 25 of your textbook
to answer the questions.

**Unification of Germany
1865–1871**

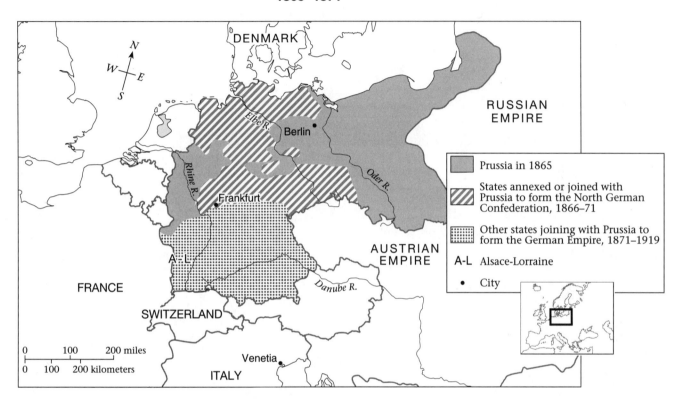

1. In 1866, Prussia fought and won a 7-week war with

   what neighbor? _____

2. In 1867, Prussia formed the North German Confederation. What city lay on the

   southern border of the North German Confederation? _____

3. In 1870, Prussia started a war with France. Prussia took the provinces of Alsace
   and Lorraine from France. What nation borders Alsace and Lorraine to the south?

   _____

4. The German Empire included all the shaded and patterned areas on the map. The German
   Empire came into being in 1871. What empires lay east of the German Empire?

   _____     _____

© Pearson Education, Inc., publishing as Globe Fearon.
All rights reserved.

# 25 ▶ Solving a Puzzle

**Exercise 66**

*Critical Thinking*

Unscramble the letters to form each answer. The circled letters will form your *final answer*.

1. The "Sword" of Italy:   b i a r a g i l d

   _ _ _ _ Ⓞ _ Ⓞ _ _

2. He took the Italian Peninsula in 1796:   p a l o o n e n

   _ _ _ Ⓞ _ Ⓞ _

3. A band of men who fought for a free Italy:   e d r   r i s h s t

   _ _ Ⓞ   _ _ _ _ _ _

4. The "Soul" of Italy:   z i a m z i n

   _ _ _ _ _ _ Ⓞ

5. Nation that met defeat in a 7-week war:   s u t i a r a

   _ _ _ _ Ⓞ _ _

6. The capital of unified Italy:   m e r o

   _ Ⓞ _ _

7. Otto von Bismarck was one:   h e r l a c n o c l

   _ _ _ Ⓞ _ _ _ _ _

*Final Answer:*
Bismarck's policy for a united Germany:

_ _ _ _ _ and _ _ _ _

© Pearson Education, Inc., publishing as Globe Fearon. All rights reserved.

## 26 ▶ Distinguishing Causes and Results

**Exercise 67**

**A.** Decide if each of the following statements describes a *cause* of World War I or a *result* of the war. Write *C* before each statement that describes a cause. Write *R* before each statement that describes a result.

_____ **1.** Nations formed alliances and promised to protect each other.

_____ **2.** France wanted to get back the provinces of Alsace and Lorraine.

_____ **3.** Germany lost all of its colonies and had to return Alsace and Lorraine to France.

_____ **4.** Germany promised to disarm.

_____ **5.** Russia had border disputes with Austria-Hungary.

_____ **6.** Arab lands once ruled by Turks fell under British control.

_____ **7.** A Serbian sniper assassinated Austrian Archduke Ferdinand.

_____ **8.** The League of Nations was established.

_____ **9.** Nations raced to build the best arms and the strongest armies.

_____ **10.** Nearly eight million soldiers died.

**B.** Write a sentence describing the result of the following group of events.

**a.** A German submarine torpedoed and sank the *Lusitania*. Among the 1,198 people who died, there were 128 Americans.

**b.** German submarines sank several American merchant ships.

**c.** U.S. President Woodrow Wilson said it was time to "make the world safe for democracy."

**Result:** _____

_____

_____

_____

© Pearson Education, Inc., publishing as Globe Fearon. All rights reserved.

**Defining Words/Writing an Opinion**                    **Exercise 68**

**A.** On April 1, 1917, President Woodrow Wilson addressed the United
States Congress. He had finally decided that the United States should
join the Allies. Read this portion of Wilson's speech. Then write a
definition for each word that is written in italics. You may use a
dictionary if you need help.

"The present German *submarine* warfare against *commerce* is a warfare
against mankind… *Neutrality* is no longer possible or desirable where
the peace of the world is involved… The world must be made safe
for democracy. There are, it may be, many months of fiery trial and
*sacrifice* ahead of us… We shall fight for the things which we have
always carried nearest our hearts—for democracy, for the right of
those who *submit* to *authority* to have a voice in their own government,
for the rights of liberties of small nations,… to make the world itself
at last free."

**1.** submarine:

_____

**2.** commerce:

_____

**3.** neutrality:

_____

**4.** sacrifice:

_____

**5.** submit:

_____

**6.** authority:

_____

**B.** President Wilson said, "The world must be made safe for democracy."
Do you think the world is "safe for democracy" today? On a separate
sheet of paper, write a paragraph stating your opinion and supporting
that opinion with facts. Give examples of current events that show
that the world is or is not safe for democracy.

© Pearson Education, Inc., publishing as Globe Fearon.
All rights reserved.

## 26 ▸ Creating a Poster

Once the United States joined the Allies in World War I, the U.S. government wanted to encourage citizens to support the war effort. Americans were asked to volunteer for the armed services. Americans at home were encouraged to plant victory gardens to provide food for the soldiers. They were called on to make sacrifices for those fighting overseas. For example, they were asked to save flour and meat for the soldiers by observing "wheatless Mondays" and "meatless Tuesdays."

The U.S. Congress set up a special government agency to "sell" the public on the war. It was called the *Committee on Public Information.* Patriotic posters appeared on the walls of public buildings.

**As a member of the Committee on Public Information, you have been asked to create a poster to promote patriotism. Your poster should encourage Americans to join the army, observe wheatless Mondays or meatless Tuesdays, plant a victory garden, or perform any other patriotic act. Make your poster in the space provided.**

© Pearson Education, Inc., publishing as Globe Fearon. All rights reserved.

**Placing Events in Time**                          **Exercise 70**

*Skill Practice*

**A.** The following events are not listed in order. Decide during which time period each event occurred. Write *A*, *B*, or *C* on each line. You may review Chapter 27 in your textbook if you need help.

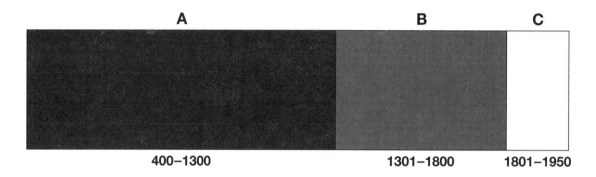

| A | B | C |
|---|---|---|
| 400–1300 | 1301–1800 | 1801–1950 |

**1.** Vikings capture Kiev. _____

**2.** Ivan the Terrible becomes first czar. _____

**3.** Russian princes defeat Mongols. _____

**4.** Vladimir I unites Kievan Russia under Eastern Orthodox Church.

_____

**5.** Russia becomes Union of Soviet Socialist Republics. _____

**6.** Batu Khan and the Mongols invade Russia. _____

**7.** Napoleon invades Russia. _____

**8.** Catherine the Great becomes ruler. _____

**9.** Workers riot on "Bloody Sunday." _____

**10.** Russian Revolution; Lenin becomes leader. _____

**B.** Choose one of the events listed above. On a separate sheet of paper, write a paragraph describing that event.

© Pearson Education, Inc., publishing as Globe Fearon. All rights reserved.

# 27 ▶ Comparing and Contrasting

**Exercise 71**

*Review*

**Write a brief paragraph to answer each item.**

**1.** What similar ideas did Peter the Great and Catherine the Great share?

_____

_____

_____

_____

**2.** Describe the major difference between Karl Marx's idea of communism and Vladimir Lenin's idea of communism.

_____

_____

_____

_____

**3.** Describe similarities in Lenin's methods of governing and Stalin's methods.

_____

_____

_____

_____

**4.** Which Russian leader do you think was the most destructive and tyrannical? Which one do you think had the most positive effect on Russia and its people? Give reasons for your choices.

_____

_____

_____

_____

© Pearson Education, Inc., publishing as Globe Fearon. All rights reserved.

# 27 ▶ Categorizing Information/Defining Words          Exercise 72

**A.** Many of the revolutionaries in Russia based their ideas about government and society on the works of the German thinker Karl Marx. Reread the section about Marx in Chapter 27. Then circle each item that describes Marx's picture of an ideal society.

> **a.** strong central government          **e.** feudalism
>
> **b.** no government          **f.** a worker's rebellion
>
> **c.** a powerful ruling class          **g.** public ownership of factories
>
> **d.** a classless society          **h.** slavery

**B.** In *The Communist Manifesto,* Karl Marx called for a worker's revolution. Marx called for the proletarians to rise up against *capitalists* and the *bourgeoisie.* He wrote:

"Working men of all countries unite!... The proletarians have nothing to lose but their chains. They have a world to win."

**You may use a dictionary to answer questions 1 to 3.**

**1.** Define *proletarians.*

_____

_____

**2.** Define *capitalists.*

_____

_____

**3.** Define *bourgeoisie.*

_____

_____

**4.** Explain what Marx meant when he said the proletarians had "nothing to lose but their chains."

_____

_____

© Pearson Education, Inc., publishing as Globe Fearon. All rights reserved.

# 28 ▸ Solving Crossword Puzzles

Use the following names to solve the puzzle.

| Historical Figures from World War II | | | | |
|---|---|---|---|---|
| Churchill | Eisenhower | Hitler | MacArthur | Mussolini |
| Rommel | Roosevelt | Tojo | Truman | |

**ACROSS**

1. German dictator

4. U.S. President throughout most of the war

6. German general called "Desert Fox"

8. British prime minister

9. U.S. President at the end of the war

**DOWN**

2. Japanese dictator

3. U.S. general who led the invasion of Normandy

5. He led U.S. forces in the Pacific.

7. Italian dictator

© Pearson Education, Inc., publishing as Globe Fearon.
All rights reserved.

# 28 ▶ Predicting What Might Have Happened

**Exercise 74**

*Critical Thinking*

**Write a brief paragraph to answer each question.**

1. In 1938, Hitler set forth on his conquest of the world. His troops took over Austria and then turned to Czechoslovakia. To keep the peace, Britain and France signed a treaty with Hitler giving him the area known as the Sudetenland. Eventually, Hitler took over the rest of Czechoslovakia. Britain and France did not declare war on Germany until the 1939 invasion of Poland. What do you think would have happened if Britain and France had declared war when Hitler first began his aggression?

   _____

   _____

   _____

   _____

   _____

   _____

   _____

2. At the beginning of World War II, the United States remained a neutral nation. It sent food and arms to Germany's enemies, but it did not get directly involved until Japan attacked Pearl Harbor. What do you think would have happened if there had never been a direct attack on the United States?

   _____

   _____

   _____

   _____

   _____

3. After the German surrender, Japan continued to fight. U.S. President Harry Truman made a difficult decision. He decided to use the atom bomb against Japan. The United States dropped two bombs, Japan surrendered, and World War II ended. What do you think would have happened if Truman had decided against using the atom bomb? Write your answer on a separate sheet of paper.

© Pearson Education, Inc., publishing as Globe Fearon. All rights reserved.

# 28 ▶ Distinguishing Causes and Results

**A.** Decide if each of the following statements describes a cause of
World War II or a result of the war. Write *C* before each statement
that describes a cause. Write *R* before each statement that describes
a result.

_____  **1.** About 55 million lives were lost.

_____  **2.** The idea of a United Nations gained support.

_____  **3.** The world learned that Hitler had set out to murder an entire
race of people.

_____  **4.** Hitler invaded Poland.

_____  **5.** Hitler, Mussolini, and Tojo all wanted to build empires.

_____  **6.** Germany was left in shambles, a totally defeated nation.

_____  **7.** Germany disregarded the Treaty of Versailles and built a mighty military.

_____  **8.** No one dared speak out against the fierce dictators who ruled
Germany, Italy, and Japan.

_____  **9.** Two Japanese cities were destroyed by atomic bombs.

_____  **10.** General Tojo was arrested and convicted as a war criminal.

**B.** Write a sentence describing the result of the following series
of events.

**a.** Russian soldiers defeated the Germans at the Battle of Stalingrad.

**b.** The Allies defeated German and Italian forces in Africa.

**c.** Allied soldiers took the beaches of Normandy and went on to free Paris.

**d.** Germans were soundly defeated in the Battle of the Bulge.

**e.** Allies invaded and took Berlin.

**Result:** _____

_____

_____

_____

© Pearson Education, Inc., publishing as Globe Fearon.
All rights reserved.

# 28 ▶ Using a Graph                                    Exercise 76

Use the graph below to answer the questions.

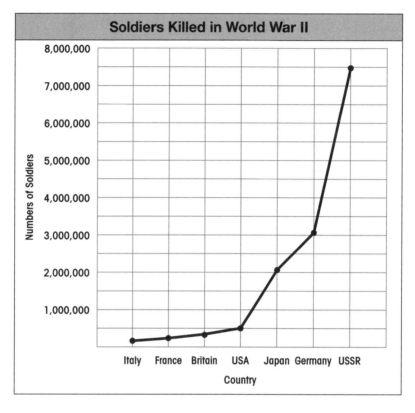

**Soldiers Killed in World War II**

1. Which country had the fewest number of soldiers killed in the war? About how many of its soldiers were killed?

   _____

2. Which country had the greatest number of soldiers killed in the war? About how many of its soldiers were killed?

   _____

3. Which countries had more than one million soldiers killed in the war?

   _____

4. Which countries lost fewer soldiers than the United States?

   _____

© Pearson Education, Inc., publishing as Globe Fearon. All rights reserved.

Name _____     Date _____

# 29 ▶ Using an Encyclopedia and an Almanac     Exercise 77

**A.** The following countries are the member nations of NATO as of
September 2000. When NATO was created by treaty in 1949, there were
12 original member nations. Use an encyclopedia or the Internet to find
out which 12 nations were charter members. Put a star (*) beside the
names of those twelve nations.

## NATO
### (North Atlantic Treaty Organization)

| | | |
|---|---|---|
| Belgium | Luxembourg | Czech Republic |
| Canada | Netherlands | Hungary |
| Denmark | France | Poland |
| Germany | Greece | |
| Iceland | Italy | |
| United States | Norway | |
| Portugal | United Kingdom | |
| Spain | Turkey | |

**B.** Review Chapter 29 in your World History textbook. Also, check an
encyclopedia, an almanac, or the Internet to read about the purpose of
NATO. Write one or two paragraphs explaining why the nations
banded together in 1949 and why they have continued and expanded
this alliance in recent times.

_____

_____

_____

_____

_____

_____

_____

_____

© Pearson Education, Inc., publishing as Globe Fearon.
All rights reserved.

# 29 ▶ Defining Words/Summarizing Information

**Exercise 78**

**A.** This is a portion of George C. Marshall's speech in support of his plan for European recovery. Read the speech. Then write the definitions of the boldfaced words. Use a dictionary if you need help.

"Europe's requirements for the next three or four years are so much greater than her present ability to pay that she must have **substantial** additional help. …

It is logical that the United States should do whatever it is able to assist in the return of normal economic health in the world, without which there can be no political **stability** or secured peace. Our policy is directed not against any country or **doctrine** but against hunger, poverty, **desperation**, and **chaos**."

substantial: _____

stability: _____

doctrine: _____

desperation: _____

chaos: _____

**B.** In a paragraph, summarize the objective of the Marshall Plan.

_____

_____

_____

_____

_____

_____

_____

_____

_____

© Pearson Education, Inc., publishing as Globe Fearon. All rights reserved.

# 29 ► Using a Map

**Exercise 79**

*Skill Practice*

Use the information in the map below to answer the questions.

### The Cold War Divides Europe, ca. 1970

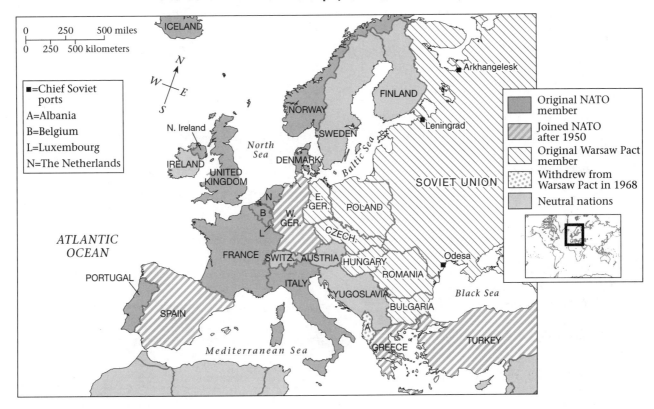

1. According to the map, which European countries joined NATO after 1950?

   _____

2. Which countries joined the Warsaw Pact? _____

   _____

3. Did Finland, Sweden, and Switzerland join an alliance? _____

   _____

4. What did Albania do in 1968? _____

5. The United States was also an original NATO member. Why do you think the

   United States joined NATO? _____

   _____

© Pearson Education, Inc., publishing as Globe Fearon.
All rights reserved.

## 30 ▶ Writing an Editorial

**Exercise 80**

*Critical Thinking*

Be a newspaper reporter in a place and time described in Chapter 30. Write an editorial giving your opinion on one of the following topics. Remember that your job is to convince your reader that your opinion is correct. Be sure to support your opinion with facts! Continue your editorial on a separate sheet of paper if you need more room.

**Suggested editorial topics:**

Apartheid

U.S. involvement in the Vietnam War

The Chinese government's response to the Tiananmen Square demonstration

U.S. involvement in Somalia

Japan's rapid industrial growth and its effect on the United States economy

_____

_____

_____

_____

_____

_____

_____

_____

_____

_____

_____

_____

© Pearson Education, Inc., publishing as Globe Fearon. All rights reserved.

# 30 ▸ Classifying Historical Topics

Each of the following words relates to one of the topic headings.
Write each word on a line under the correct heading.

| | | | |
|---|---|---|---|
| apartheid | rivalry with Pakistan | Mao Zedong | Nelson Mandela |
| Cultural Revolution | Red Guards | Indira Gandhi | ANC |
| domino theory | Ho Chi Minh | Tiananmen Square | Idi Amin |
| industrial and economic boom | Khmer Rouge | Mau Mau | boat people |
| | factory explosion | | |

### India after World War II

_____

_____

_____

### China after World War II

_____

_____

_____

### Japan after World War II

_____

_____

_____

### Southeast Asia after World War II

_____

_____

_____

### Africa after World War II

_____

_____

_____

© Pearson Education, Inc., publishing as Globe Fearon. All rights reserved.

## 31 ▶ Using a Chart

Use the chart to compare the nations of the Middle East. Then answer
the questions on the following page.

| Nation | Approx. Population | Major Religion | Capital City | Government | Head of State | Literacy Rate |
|---|---|---|---|---|---|---|
| Saudi Arabia | 22,023,506 | 100% Muslim | Riyadh | Monarchy with council of ministers | King Fahd Abdul Aziz | 63% |
| Iran | 65,619,636 | 89% Shi'a Muslim 10% Sunni Muslim | Tehran | Islamic Republic | Ayatollah Ali Hoseini-Khamenei | 79% |
| Iraq | 22,675,617 | 97% Muslim | Baghdad | Republic | Pres. Saddam Hussein | 58% |
| Turkey | 65,666,677 | 99.8% Muslim | Ankara | Republic | Pres. Ahmet Necdet Sezer | 82% |
| Syria | 16,305,659 | 74% Sunni Muslim 16% other 10% Christian | Damascus | Republic (under military regime) | Pres. al-Assad Bashar | 79% |
| Lebanon | 3,578,036 | 70% Islam 30% Christian | Beirut | Republic | Pres. Emile Lahoud | 92% |
| United Arab Emirates | 2,369,153 | 96% Muslim 4% Christian, Hindu, Other | Abu Dhabi | Federation of emirates | Pres. Zaid bin Sultan an-Nahayan | 79% |
| Yemen | 17,479,206 | 53% Sunni Muslim | Sanaa | Republic | Pres. Lt. Gen. Ali Abdullah Saleh | 43% |
| Oman | 2,533,389 | 75% Ibadhi Muslim 25% Sunni Muslim | Muscat | Absolute monarchy | Sultan Qabus bin Said | 59% |
| Egypt | 68,359,979 | 94% Muslim (mostly Sunni) 6% Coptic Orthodox Church | Cairo | Republic | Pres. Hosni Mubarak | 51% |
| Israel | 5,842,454 | 80% Judaism 15% Muslim (mostly sunni) | Jerusalem | Republic | Pres. Ezer Weizman | 96% |
| Libya | 5,115,450 | 97% Sunni Muslim | Tripoli | Islamic Arabic Socialist "Mass State" | Col. Muammar al-Qaddafi (no official title defacto) | 76% |
| Cyprus | 758,363 | 78% Greek Orthodox 18% Muslim | Nicosia | Republic | Pres. Glafcos Clerides | 95% |
| Jordan | 4,998,564 | 96% Sunni Muslim 4% Christian | Amman | Constitutional monarchy | Abdullah II | 87% |

© Pearson Education, Inc., publishing as Globe Fearon.
All rights reserved.

1. Compare the population statistics with the map on page 466 of your textbook. Which nation has a *denser* population, Iran or Saudi Arabia?

    _____

2. Which nation has a *denser* population, Egypt or Libya?

    _____

3. In which two nations does the highest percentage of the population know how to

    read and write? _____ and _____

4. Which nation has the lowest literacy rate?

    _____

5. Most of the Middle Eastern nations have what form of government?

    _____

6. Most of the people in the Middle East are members of what religion?

    _____

7. Most Israelis are members of what religion?

    _____

8. Which country has the largest population?

    _____

9. Which country has the smallest population?

    _____

10. Which country has a republic form of government but is ruled by a military regime?

    _____

© Pearson Education, Inc., publishing as Globe Fearon. All rights reserved.

# 31 ▶ Presenting Point of View

**Exercise 83**

*Critical Thinking*

**A.** The Palestinians and the Israelis view the lands that were once called Palestine from very different points of view. Eventually, those lands became Israel and Jordan, and 700,000 Palestinian Arabs became refugees.

Write one paragraph discussing the division of Palestine and the establishment of the state of Israel from an Israeli point of view. Write a second paragraph discussing the same topic from a Palestinian point of view. You may review sections of Chapter 31 if you need help.

_____

_____

_____

_____

_____

_____

_____

_____

_____

_____

_____

_____

_____

_____

_____

**B.** Look for information about the relationship between Israelis and Palestinians today. Find and read a newspaper or magazine article that tells about the two groups. Write a one-paragraph summary of the article on a separate sheet of paper.

© Pearson Education, Inc., publishing as Globe Fearon. All rights reserved.

# 31 ▶ Word Play

**Circle the correct answer in each group of phrases. Then put the answers together, sound them out, and they will help you come up with a final answer. Write the final answer on the line. (The final answers are all terms that can be found in Chapter 31.)**

1. A king and queen live in one:
   mansion    palace    hut

2. The prong on a fork:
   tine    blade    bowl

   **Final answer**—Both Arabs and Jews considered this place their homeland:

   _____

3. An owl's favorite question:
   what?    who?    where?

4. The opposite of crazy:
   sane    friendly    lonely

   **Final answer**—the Iraqi leader who invaded Kuwait:

   _____

5. Opposite of happy:
   joyful    greedy    sad

6. It sits on top of an "i":
   square    comma    dot

   **Final answer**—an Egyptian president who worked for peace:

   _____

7. To rip apart:
   mend    glue    tear

8. A lion's sound:
   bark    tweet    roar

9. They hold your hands onto your arms:
   ankles    wrists    shoulders

   **Final answer**—those who use random violence to get what they want:

   _____

© Pearson Education, Inc., publishing as Globe Fearon. All rights reserved.

# 32 ▶ Looking at History Through Journalism       Exercise 85

*Critical Thinking*

**A.** Today's newspapers often report news about Russia or other nations that were once part of the Soviet Union. Find a current events story about one of these nations. Write a summary of the article on the lines below. Then attach the article to this page.

_____

_____

_____

_____

_____

_____

_____

_____

_____

_____

_____

_____

_____

_____

**B.** You are a newspaper reporter. You are on the spot for a firsthand look at the breakup of the Soviet Union and the other sweeping changes in Eastern Europe in the late 1980s and early 1990s. On a separate sheet of paper, write a news article for one of these headlines. You may need to get some more information from an encyclopedia, or an almanac, or the Internet to write your article.

**COUP FAILS, SOVIET CITIZENS SAY "NO" TO COMMUNISM**

**BERLIN WALL FALLS, EAST GERMANS STREAM TO WEST**

**YUGOSLAV BREAKUP LEADS TO CIVIL WAR**

© Pearson Education, Inc., publishing as Globe Fearon. All rights reserved.

**Understanding Responsibility in the World**   **Exercise 86**

**Read each numbered item below and follow the directions.**

1. Many changes have taken place in Russia in recent years. Do you think the United States should help Russia to improve its economy? Why or why not?

   _____

   _____

   _____

   _____

   _____

   _____

2. After Yugoslavia broke up, the United States took part in NATO-led efforts to bring peace to the region. Do you think the United States has a responsibility to help keep peace in Europe? Why or why not?

   _____

   _____

   _____

   _____

   _____

   _____

3. On a separate sheet of paper, write a letter to our President explaining your position as a U.S. citizen.

© Pearson Education, Inc., publishing as Globe Fearon.
All rights reserved.

Name _____  Date _____

# 33 ▶ Debating an Issue                           **Exercise 87**

*Critical Thinking*

Your debate topic is:

### *"Resolved: the United States has a duty to 'protect' the Western Hemisphere"*

Some of the statements listed below support the *pro* side of the debate. They imply that the United States must involve itself in civil conflict of Latin American nations or defend against threats against those nations. Other statements support the *con* side of the debate, suggesting that the United States should stay out of Latin American affairs.

**Decide if each statement is for (pro) or against (con) the resolution.
Write *pro* or *con*.**

_____ **1.** A Communist threat against any nation in the Western Hemisphere is a threat against the United States.

_____ **2.** The United States cannot police the world.

_____ **3.** The United States has its own problems of poverty, homelessness, unemployment, racial strife, and economic recession. The government must use its energies and resources at home.

_____ **4.** The United States was founded on the principles of democracy and must defend those principles in its own hemisphere.

_____ **5.** The United States cannot allow enemy military bases in the Americas.

_____ **6.** The United States has a moral duty to take action when people are treated inhumanely and are denied basic rights.

_____ **7.** No American should be asked to risk his or her life fighting a foreign war.

_____ **8.** Americans cannot impose their values on the peoples of other nations.

_____ **9.** Consider what happened in Europe before World War II. Britain and France failed to act against German aggression until it was too late!

_____ **10.** Like dominoes, if Latin American nations fall to the enemy, the United States will eventually be in danger too.

© Pearson Education, Inc., publishing as Globe Fearon. All rights reserved.

Name _____  Date _____

## 33 ▶ Classifying Nations/Making a Graph    Exercise 88

*Skill Practice*

**A.** Circle the item in each category that does not belong. Review Chapter 33 in your textbook if you need help. For more help, use a map of the Western Hemisphere or the world. A useful map is on page 302 of your textbook.

1. Central American nations:

   Nicaragua    Panama    Brazil    El Salvador

2. South American nations:

   Chile    Colombia    Peru    Haiti

3. Nations of the Caribbean:

   Jamaica    Haiti    Bolivia    Cuba

4. Island nations:

   Suriname    Grenada    Barbados    Dominican Republic

5. Nations that received U.S. military aid in the 1980s:

   Nicaragua    El Salvador    Grenada    Argentina

6. Major problems in Mexico:

   earthquakes    pollution    flooding    rapid population growth

7. Latin American leaders:

   Fidel Castro    Margaret Thatcher    Daniel Ortega    Vicente Fox Quesada

8. Partners in a 1992 free-trade agreement:

   Argentina    United States    Mexico    Canada

9. Non-Communist nations in Latin America:

   Cuba    Mexico    Brazil    Peru

**B.** Tourism is an important part of the economy of some Latin American countries. On a separate sheet of paper, make a bar graph showing the following information.

**Tourist industry in some Latin American nations.**

Brazil: $3.99 billion

Mexico: $7.59 billion

Argentina: $2.81 billion

Chile: $1.06 billion

Costa Rica: $1 billion

© Pearson Education, Inc., publishing as Globe Fearon. All rights reserved.

Chapter 33 • Latin America After World War II    89

# 34 ▸ Comparing Your Culture's Past and Present     Exercise 89

**A.** Different cultures are characterized by their customs and traditions. Yet as time passes, some of those customs and traditions change. Describe changes that have occurred in your own culture in the following areas.

**1.** the role of women: _____

_____

_____

**2.** family life: _____

_____

_____

**3.** education: _____

_____

_____

**4.** relations with people of other cultures: _____

_____

_____

**5.** religion and society: _____

_____

_____

**B.** On a separate sheet of paper, write a paragraph describing some customs and traditions of your culture that have *not* changed very much throughout the years.

© Pearson Education, Inc., publishing as Globe Fearon. All rights reserved.

**Thinking About Technology**                    **Exercise 90**

**A.** Technology develops as the years pass. Describe changes that have occurred during your own lifetime in each of the following fields. Tell how those changes have affected your own life.

**1.** space travel: _____

_____

_____

_____

_____

**2.** computers: _____

_____

_____

_____

_____

**3.** health care and medicine: _____

_____

_____

_____

_____

**4.** industry: _____

_____

_____

_____

_____

**B.** Choose one of the fields listed in Part A. On a separate sheet of paper, write a paragraph predicting future advances in that field. (For example, what will space travel be like in 2093? *or* What role will computers play in future society?)

© Pearson Education, Inc., publishing as Globe Fearon. All rights reserved.

Name _____  Date _____

## 34 ▶ Using a Chart

Use the chart below to answer the questions. Then circle the one best answer. To understand the chart, you will need to learn or review the following terms:

**Literacy:** the percentage of the population that can read and write

**Gross domestic product:** total value of all final goods and services produced in a country in a year

**Per Capita GDP:** the gross domestic product of a country divided by the number of people in that country

| Some Developed and Less Developed Countries | | | |
|---|---|---|---|
| **Developed Countries** | **Literacy** | **Gross Domestic Product (GDP)** | **Per Capita GDP** |
| Canada | 97% | 688.3 billion | 22,400 |
| France | 99% | 1.32 trillion | 22,600 |
| Germany | 100% | 1.81 trillion | 22,100 |
| Israel (Literacy) | 96% | 101.9 billion | 18,100 |
| Japan | 100% | 2.9 trillion | 23,100 |
| United States | 97% | $8.51 trillion | $31,500 |
| United Kingdom | 100% | 1.252 trillion (Per Capita GDP) | 21,200 |
| **Developing Countries** | **Literacy** | **GDP** | **Per Capita GDP** |
| Afghanistan | 31.5% | 20 billion | 800 |
| Bangladesh | 38% | 175.5 billion | 1,380 |
| Cambodia | 65% | 7.8 billion | 700 |
| India | 52% | 1.689 trillion | 1,720 |
| Nicaragua | 66% | 11.6 billion | 2,500 |
| Nigeria | 57% | 106.2 billion | 960 |
| Peru | 89% | 111.8 billion | 4,300 |
| Saudi Arabia | 63% | 186 billion | 9,000 |
| Somalia | 24% | 4 billion | 600 |

1.  Which statement best describes a developed nation?

    **(a)** Half of the people are literate.   **(b)** Nearly all of the people are literate.   **(c)** Very few of the people are literate.

2.  India has a fairly high gross domestic product. Yet the per capita gross domestic product is below $2,000. What does this tell you about India?

    **(a)** It is a highly developed country.   **(b)** It has a very large population.   **(c)** Most of the people cannot read or write.

3.  Saudi Arabia is rich in oil deposits. This fact would explain why:

    **(a)** It has a fairly high per capita GDP.   **(b)** Over one-fourth of its population is illiterate.   **(c)** It is a less developed nation.

4.  Developing nations on the chart are found in which three parts of the world?

    **(a)** Europe, North America, and Asia   **(b)** Asia, Europe, and Latin America   **(c)** Latin America, Africa, and Asia

© Pearson Education, Inc., publishing as Globe Fearon. All rights reserved.